MOTIVATED OR MISPLACED?

8 Steps to Create
the Life That You Want!

Table of Contents

Introduction

What it Means to be "Motivated or Misplaced"
Foreword by Les Brown — 6
About the Author — 7
Dedications and Acknowledgements
Preface — 9

Part One | Rediscover Your Passion and Purpose

Chapter 1: **The One Word That Defines Your Life** — 12
Chapter 2: **Are You Motivated or Misplaced?** — 15
Chapter 3: **Introduction to Your New Life** — 18
Chapter 4: **Living Life on Your Terms** — 21

Part Two | How Did You End Up Here?

Chapter 5: **The Conventional Path is an Illusion** — 28
Chapter 6: **Traits You Learned That Hold You Back** — 34
Chapter 7: **Traits That You Should Have Learned** — 43

Part Three | 8 Steps to Create the Life That You Want!

Chapter 8: Step 1: **Visualize That It's Yours** — 58
Chapter 9: Step 2: **Invest in Yourself** — 64
Chapter 10: Step 3: **Create the Right Goals** — 75
Chapter 11: Step 4: **Think Like an Entrepreneur** — 82
Chapter 12: Step 5: **Own Your Financial Future** — 102
Chapter 13: Step 6: **Embrace Change** — 119

Chapter 14: Step 7: **Serve Others to Reach Success**   129

Chapter 15: Step 8: **Internalize Perseverance**   136

Part Four | **THE PATH AHEAD**

Chapter 16:   **Coping with Misplaced People**   142

A Message from the Author: "**Sorry, You're Two Pennies Short**"   145

Additional Reading & Planning Apps   148

Bibliography   149

What it Means to Be "Motivated or Misplaced?"

In one of the most famous novels in modern history, "The Death of Ivan Ilych," the lead character, Ivan, upon his deathbed, asks this question, "What if my whole life has been wrong?" You see, up until the brink of his death, Ivan was living someone else's life. His career was one that others thought he should have. His pursuits in life were based on the person that he thought he needed to be. He had a good life; it just wasn't the one that he knew in his heart he should have lived. He ultimately died with his passions and purpose still inside, untapped, and hidden. The gifts that he took to his grave, would have dramatically changed not only Ivan's life, but also those of many other people that he would have touched along the way.

What if you asked yourself that same question right now? What would the answer be for you? **Are you truly living the life that you want? Or, are you living the life that you or someone else thought that you should have?**

If you aren't living the life that you want, then you're Misplaced. Whatever you're doing is not what you should be doing. It's not what you want to be doing, and it's not what you showed up here to do. Thanks to an outdated educational system, peer pressure, lack of courage, and a variety of other factors, there are generations of people who have spent their entire life Misplaced, only to regret it in the end, when it's too late to do anything about it. You must not allow this to happen to you.

The life that you are living is the only one that you're going to get. Do you want to use it living for something other than your true passion and purpose? Do you want to be full of regret at the end – flooded with thoughts of the things that you should have done?

Remember those famous words of wisdom from Randy Pausch, in his "Last Lecture":

> **"It's not the things we do in life that we regret on our deathbed. It's the things that we did not do."**

Do you believe that there should be more to your life, but you just don't know where to begin? Do you sometimes wish that somebody would take the time to encapsulate the major things that you need to learn in order get started?

If you're ready, then you're in the right place right now. This book will first help clarify what you want your ideal life to look like, and then help you establish a game plan on how to get there. The rest is up to you, but if you're hungry for change, you can make it happen. If you've found this book early in your life, at a time when you're thinking about the path that you will choose for the next 5-10 years, then you're fortunate because it could save you from years of being Misplaced. You will soon realize that much of what you've learned up until now is actually counter-intuitive to help you reach the outcome that you want. If you are well into your journey but on the wrong path, then you need it even more.

The goal is for you to have a truly <u>Motivated</u> life. One where you live life on your terms! You're in charge, and your significant life decisions are made by you, not for you. "Motivated or Misplaced" is about this journey. First, it illustrates some of the things that may have led you to the wrong path. You will see that the majority of reasons for living a Misplaced life emanate from ineffective skills and traits that were taught to you many years ago. After briefly pointing out some things that may have put you on the wrong path, the majority of the book takes you through eight steps that will help reposition you for the right path, one that you design based on your unique passion and purpose. Whether you're just starting out, or looking for a fresh beginning, this book is meant to help you create a new blueprint for your life -- one that you can use to create your own Motivated life.

"Motivated or Misplaced" is a gift for you and to you. After reading it and using its information to create the right outcome for your life, you will be able to take your success to an even higher level, and you'll be equipped to help others do the same. There is no greater feeling of accomplishment than living the life that you were meant to live, and then also helping others achieve the same. Congratulations on taking the first important step!

Onward...

Foreword by Les Brown

I got a call from my granddaughter and I could hear in her voice that she'd been crying. I asked, what's the matter, Cleopatra? She said, grandpa, my boss is just getting on my last nerve, I'm not supposed to be here, I can't stand this job; but it pays the bills. I gave her a few words of encouragement and said, you won't be there long because you're not in your true place. She was working a job that paid the bills, but she realized being my granddaughter, that you were not born to work for a living but to live your making, and living you're making will make your living.

My name is Les Brown. I've come to believe in life, that wherever you are is your rightful place, your rightful place is where your thoughts have brought you; your true place is where your thoughts can take you.

Daren Benzi, father, speaker, global business consultant and creative author has written a book that is designed to help you live a larger life, to tap into your greatness, to conquer your fears and ultimately to get unstuck and live the life that you were born to live. The book that Daren has written is a book that I feel addresses a major challenge that many people are facing, which he calls, the **Misplaced life.** We are in an era that the late Peter Drucker calls the three C's: accelerated change, overwhelming complexity, and tremendous competition. For the most part, our educational system has not prepared us with the right mindset or skillset for this era. We need new strategies and skills to help us prepare for a life that gives us a sense of meaning and fulfillment.

Daren is not only a messenger, but he lives the message that he brings. His life is an example which demonstrates that at any given time, we can redefine how we see ourselves. Daren has given us the blueprint for living the **Motivated life**. He lays out in detail the process of how you can master change in your life and reach beyond yourself. If you're a young person getting out of school or a person in mid-career stuck between your dream and a job like my granddaughter, this book will allow you to liberate yourself.

Daren Benzi, raised in a single mother household and living in a mobile home made a conscious decision not to allow his environment and the adversities in life define who he would become. Driven by hunger to live a purposeful, passionate life, he literally soared to an executive suite in Manhattan, becoming a dominant voice in the global business space. Now, a highly sought-after consultant for major corporations around the world, Daren's fresh perspective on success, motivation, and life-changing tactics is destined to catapult him as a voice of transformation for many years to come. Daren Benzi walks his talk.

It has been said, the wealthiest place on the planet is not in the Middle East, where there is oil in the ground, and, it's not in South Africa, with its diamond mines. Dr. Myles Munroe, a great orator from the Bahamas said, "the wealthiest place in the planet is the cemetery." The cemetery is filled with people who lived Misplaced lives with their gifts, abilities, talents, and skills that they took with them to their graves. With each word in this book, Daren Benzi challenges you to get out of your head and get into your greatness. He inspires you to step out of line, not follow the crowd, but instead, find your own true passion and purpose. He challenges you to operate in the thinking of Henry David Thoreau, who said, "Do not go where the path may lead but go where there's no path and leave a trail." You have something special, you have greatness within you, there is a place for you. Now it's time for you to find your true place and live the life that you were chosen to live.

When you have finished reading this book, your life will never be the same. That's my story and I'm sticking to it.

About the Author:

Daren Benzi is an attorney, author, business consultant, investor, and speaker. He has worked as a policy lawyer for the Federal Communications Commission in Washington DC, has been a top corporate executive generating hundreds of millions of dollars in revenue for a major global media company, led new business development and strategy for the president of a major television network, and led global marketing and business development for one of the largest tech start-ups in Silicon Valley. Today, Daren serves as an independent business consultant helping CEOs and other senior level executives formulate creative business strategies to fuel growth and innovation. Daren is also an avid investor and speaker. Daren believes that if people live their passion and purpose and bring their gifts to the surface, they will literally change their own life, and the lives of those around them. His most important role is that of dad.

Dedication:

For my sons, Dylan and Blake. This book is for you! You are my greatest contribution to the world. May you always live life on your terms, and may you find your passion and purpose early, and keep those gifts with you throughout your life.

Acknowledgements:

Thank you to Nina Sandman for the countless hours that she put into reviewing and editing this work. It made a huge difference!

Thank you also to all the successful people in the world that have taken the time to write or speak about their individual journey, so that others may learn from them, and advance their own.

A special note of gratitude to three, that in this author's opinion are the best that this world has ever seen: **Les Brown, Wayne Dyer and Tony Robbins.**

Preface:

"The way we choose to see the world creates the world we see."

~ Barry Neil Kaufman

You're either living a life of passion and purpose, which is a Motivated life, or one of submission and servitude, which is a Misplaced life. Ultimately, it's not any more complicated than that. Many of us move back and forth between these two pillars frequently throughout our lives. Some, unfortunately, remain "Misplaced" for their entire life and end up looking back with enormous regret. This book is about making sure that doesn't happen to you.

Whether this book was given to you by somebody, or whether it caught your attention, the universe is speaking to you on some level. There's something inside of you that wants to come out. Most likely, you're not on the path that you envisioned for your life. Whether you're a student just starting out in life, or a mid-career professional, you will learn that by following a few key strategies, you can dramatically change your mindset, your path, and in turn, your life. Yes, you can be the person you were meant to be. The alternative is to continue following the crowd and the conventional path, and thus end up in the wrong place in your life -- Misplaced.

What Does Misplaced Mean?

- **Living your life for others**. Always making the decisions you think others want you to make, instead of the decisions that you know are right for you.
- **Ignoring your passions**. Not doing what you really want to do, while you continue doing what you were taught is the right thing.
- **Living without financial peace of mind**. You cannot have the life that you truly want without having a written financial plan to follow.
- **Pursuing the conventional path**. Following a path only because it seems like the most logical way for you to earn a living, even though in many cases, that same path prevents you from creating a happy life.
- **Living a life largely dependent upon others for your success.** Placing your peace of mind, income and happiness in someone else's hands, instead of creating and living life on your terms.

Is this the life you are living? If so, then the only way to change it is to take action and create a new plan right now! The strategies in this book will help you create and live the life that you want -- a Motivated life.

YOU own your life and can live it on your own terms. This doesn't mean that you should avoid following certain logical rules or throw caution to the wind and quit what you're doing now. It also doesn't mean that you won't face any problems along the way in achieving your Motivated life. Living life on your terms means that you are creating your own way, one that is designed by you, for you. What could be better than that? It means that you will create and follow your own blueprint, and not try to make someone else's version of your life fit you. You will know your path and plan, and you'll have a strong sense of where it will lead you. Best of all, after you've done the work on your own life, you will serve as an inspiration to others, and can help them do the same – reach a Motivated life.

What Does Motivated Mean?

- **A life where you're in charge of your future.** You aren't entirely dependent upon others for your needs and desires.
- **A life of passion and purpose.** In some way, you are contributing to the world through your innate gifts.
- **A life that that is built on pursuing your dreams.** No matter what others think, you're going after what you want.
- **Being the CEO of you!** You're the boss of you.
- **Feeling secure in your financial future.** Knowing that you have a plan to follow that makes sense and serves you well long-term.
- **Believing in the person that is best suited to design your future—You!** Because it's true.

How to Experience this Book:

The first part of this book is about rediscovering your passion and purpose.

"You had a purpose before anyone had an opinion."

~ Anonymous

The book begins with a brief introduction and imaginary journey to your new life. Your Motivated life. As with any successful journey, it's always best to start by thinking about the desired outcome before you begin. Asking yourself how you define success. Before you move too far into the book, you need to do this necessary step.

Next, the book spends a few moments looking at where you are now, and highlights some of the things that may have contributed to your current state. While these are things that you probably never think about, they are likely firmly implanted in your subconscious mind. For example, when you go to a new place (it could be a restaurant, library, store or concert) where there are a lot of people around you, do you still sit passively without talking to those around you? Do you feel most comfortable when following very specific directions? Does it make you feel uncomfortable when you're doing something different and not following the group? Might it be that acting this way is the result of a trained behavior from the early days of your education? Unfortunately, you've likely been taught a set of traits that were once ideal for making you a great employee for the industrial era, but are no longer serving you well in today's information age. Your formal educational experience probably filled you with a lot of knowledge, which, in and of itself, is not a bad thing. Knowledge alone, however, won't change your life. It must be coupled with action and execution in order for you to succeed in today's competitive environment.

Ironically, many of the passive traits that you learned in school are actually now being programmed into robots, which will replace the very human employees relying on those same traits to earn a living today. This entire book could focus on the future of robotics in the workplace, but this is not the goal. Suffice is to say, that in order to get to where you want to go, you might have to unlearn certain things in addition to learning new strategies. In some instances, unlearning can be just as important, or even more important than learning, especially when you want to create change in your life. Next, the book briefly looks at several traits that you will need to learn (if you don't already know them) in order to be successful and live a Motivated life. These traits include things like how to set goals, think creatively, be competitive, and how to influence and lead others.

Finally, you will move into the 8 Steps that will help propel you to reach a Motivated life. At first, you will be confronted with a challenge to commit to creating the necessary change. The book begins with helping you focus on changing your mind. All change begins within, and works its way out into the physical world around you. Then, there's the challenge to stay committed to the change, by investing in you. That isn't always easy, but it always produces dividends. The journey then moves to helping you design the right goals for you. This is key because on the days of your greatest challenges as your goals will keep you focused and driven. Then, you will be asked to adopt a new mindset, and to start thinking like an entrepreneur. Having the right mindset is crucial for success. Your journey then continues by looking at some simple steps that you can take to design your financial future. No successful life can be created without having financial peace of mind. Having a written plan will help you achieve this goal.

The remainder of the book is about persevering and helping others. It's hard to go back to old habits when you have others depending upon you to teach them your successful and stronger new habits. Keep in mind as you read through the chapters that, ultimately, it is the outcome that you're after, and not the comfort or lack thereof in getting there. If you move one step forward each day and stay consistent, results will come. Even small steps are progress. The universe simply has to respond to that type of determination. You will end up with a new life, one owned by you and one that you will recognize and experience as a Motivated life.

Let's begin!

Part One: Rediscover Your Passion and Purpose

~

Chapter 1:

The One Word That Defines Your Life

"Whatever you put up with, you end up with."

~ Anonymous

This book contains a transformational message, and life-changing strategies. However, the only way to bring them to life and make them work for you, is to change your thinking and your actions. It won't be easy, but it is simple. Right now, in your life, your results, or the outcomes from any efforts that you've made, are in direct proportion to what you have subconsciously decided to accept. Your brain has been programmed to establish your comfort zone at this current level in your life. As of this moment, you consciously or subconsciously feel that the pain of growing further would be greater than the pain that you feel from remaining where you are.

This can be summed up in one word, and this one word is ruining your life. What is the word, you ask?

~ TOLERATE ~

Tolerate is defined in Webster's dictionary as follows:

"To allow the existence, or practice of (something that one does not necessarily like or agree with) without interference."

"To accept or endure (someone or something, unpleasant or disliked) with forbearance."

When you think about your life today, what have you decided to tolerate? Over the years, how many things have you wished you could change, but ultimately accepted without attempting to change them? Championship football coach Mike Ditka said it best, when he said:

"In life, we get what we tolerate."

If you want this book to work for you, then you must, absolutely must, change what you are willing to tolerate. You have to raise your standards. You have to convince your brain that the pain of tolerating your current life is greater than the pain that you will face by changing. To change what you will tolerate, first take a step back and look at the big picture surrounding your life. Ask yourself what things exist in your life today that you wish you could change? Do you have enough money to live the life that you want? Are you physically fit and full of energy? Do you have great relationships, both personal and professional? Are you happy with your goals, your recent results, and the direction that your life is heading? Whatever your answers are to these questions, you will quickly see that where you are is subconsciously or consciously where you think you should be.

Where you are now is comfortable and safe in your mind. And yet, you know that in your heart that there's something more! "Motivated or Misplaced" is based on the idea that you need to get out of your mind, and into your heart. Once you do that, and truly listen to your heart, you will start moving quickly toward the things that you really want, based on your true passion and purpose. Your heart will lead you well past what you've tolerated thus far, if you listen and take action! Once you do this, the mind has no choice but to follow and to make your new life a reality.

Learn to view the word "Tolerate" with disdain. Starting today, you will no longer tolerate things that aren't in sync with the life that you want, a truly Motivated life. You will have the courage to raise your standards and to pursue your dreams!

Motivated Thinking from Chapter 1

- Whatever you put up with, you end up with.
- Whatever you "Tolerate," you become.
- Change your life by changing what you tolerate.
- What do you tolerate, that you know you should not?

Chapter 2:

Are You Motivated or Misplaced?

"If you do not change direction, you may end up where you are heading."

~Lao Tzu

"Ladies and gentlemen, this is your pilot speaking. I realize that you boarded this flight in New York and that you wish to end up in California. I'll do my very best to get you there. Today, we're operating without a flight plan, and our instruments aren't working. However, the weather looks great outside our window and we know that if we head west, there's a good chance that we'll find California at some point."

How confident would you be in that trip? The only things that the pilot really knows is where she is now, and that at the immediate location, the weather looks good. But, she has no idea how to really reach the end result – arrival in California.

Where are you in your life's journey? Are you better equipped than the pilot to achieve your desired end result? Do you even know what that end result looks like? What is your plan and strategy to get you there? Most people are so caught up in the busyness of their daily lives, that they fail to plan for the life that they truly want.

Never get so busy making a living that you forget to make a life!

The key is to learn the new strategies outlined herein, and then take action to change course. You must make sure that you have every advantage working for you so that you achieve the desired outcome. What is the desired outcome, you ask? That's something that you have to answer for yourself.

Where are you right now in your life? Are you in a place where you feel in control of your future? Are you serving as an example and helping others achieve their own greatness? If you're reading this, chances are great that there is something you believe should change, and that's a very good thing. Change comes from moving beyond your current circumstances. Where you will end up is a far better place.

Is there one area of your life where you feel that things are working as they should? Perhaps your commitment to fitness has you in the type of physical shape that you're proud of, and you are encouraged by your progress. Or, maybe you're not in great physical shape but your career is hugely successful. Is there an area of your life where you've already reached the Motivated stage? If so, that's the model for other areas. If there are no areas in your life right now where you feel successful, then you need to achieve at least one very soon.

The famous philosopher Socrates was right when he said, "The unexamined life is not worth living." How often do you really think about your life? Do you have a real and thoughtful answer when asked what you want from your life? Let's start by responding to the one basic question that most people fear:

What Do You Really Want from Your Life?

If you do nothing more than think through and determine what you really want from your life, you will already be vastly ahead of the crowd and on the right path to attaining it. The universe will begin to work with you to bring the people, opportunities and circumstances into your life in order to help make it happen.

At this early stage of imagining the life that you want, thinking about how you will actually achieve it isn't necessary and it shouldn't be your primary concern. As my friend Les Brown often says, "the how is none of your business." The most important thing right now is to think about the life that you really want, and to hold onto that vision. Soon you'll begin to see it as though you already have it – that's when change occurs.

Motivated Thinking from Chapter 2:

- The only way to reach your destination is to have a plan on how to get there.
- Living life according to someone else's rules leads to unfulfilled dreams.
- You can change your life today.

- You can live the life that you want, but you must first clearly define what that means.
- If you don't change anything, will your life change?

Chapter 3:

Introduction to Your New Life

"It's never too late to be what you might have been."

~ George Elliot

Think about the following scenario. Your friend bought you a lottery ticket and, as luck would have it, you won. You now have enough money to do whatever you want, instead of what you must. What would you do to find fulfillment in your life? After the trips and the fun, what would get you out of bed in the morning? Whatever your answer may be, the odds are very good that it's tied to your life's true passion and purpose. Now that you've thought about this, here's the million-dollar question, why aren't you doing that now? Even if you can't do it as your career, then why aren't you doing it in addition to your career?

The reason that the title of this book grabbed your attention is because you know that there's something more waiting for you. You've felt it pulling at your insides for a while now and today is the day that you begin to figure out what it might be. You want to bring whatever it is to the surface and make it part of your life from now on.

You're in the right place to find a new beginning, a new path. The path that part of you knows you should have been on from the start. Or, if you're just starting out, the unconventional path that leads to far a better outcome. If you're in the wrong place now, it just means that somewhere in life, you went left, instead of right. At some point, you did what you were conditioned to do, instead of what you should have done. And now, like so many others, you're searching for a new life, the one that's been inside of you all along, but hasn't been allowed to become your reality. This is the life that you think about at night when your world is quiet, and it's just you and your inner voice communicating. There's a famous quote by Rumi that sums this up:

"What you seek is also seeking you."

Starting today, you will pay attention to what is seeking you. You still need to learn some new things to help you do that, so keep reading. New results can be refreshing and energizing, especially if you've been in a continuous cycle of activity, only to end up in the same place. You can get the results that you are meant to achieve. You were sent here with a purpose and a unique set of gifts, and it's precisely your purpose and gifts that will fuel the change that you seek. You need to learn how to make it happen. And, you will.

The real tragedy that nobody seems to talk about is that a majority of the people in the world are living as though this life is merely a rehearsal. These people merely exist. They work. They worry about bills. They try their best to raise smart, capable, loving children. But along the way, they sacrifice who they are and their purpose on this earth. To make matters worse, parents, along with the archaic educational systems, end up passing this way of thinking on to the next generation, and the pattern repeats. All the while, people move further and further away from their individual passions and purpose to a life of mere servitude. And, it truly doesn't have to be this way. The road out of this type of life runs right through the center of your mind. You must change your thinking to change your life. It's not easy, but it is simple!

So, why take the time and make the investment in your new life? Because, years from now when you look back on this pivotal time, you will be proud of the fact that you took action and created real and lasting change. Your life won't be ordinary, you won't live for a tomorrow that never comes, and you won't reach the end and feel like you never began. No, your new life, starting right now, is about making sure that every chapter from this point forward is built by you, for you. Selfishly, this is your gift to yourself. You're going to take the time to set things up the way that you want them and ultimately, you will live a life that you can be proud of, and one that inspires others.

> **"Change is hard at first, messy in the middle and gorgeous at the end."**
>
> **~ Robin Sharma**

The key thing to think about is what your life might look like next month, next week and next year. Imagine, who you will be then. Think about pursuing your passion and purpose, having goals, investing in yourself, having your finances under control and helping others achieve their own dreams. This can be your reality in your new life. It's time to leave this one behind. You are the star now of your own movie so go ahead and make it a smashing success!

Motivated Thinking from Chapter 3:

- Your new life begins today.
- Starting now, you're going to focus on you, your passion and purpose.
- You will create a new path for you as a gift to yourself.
- You will live a life that you're proud of, and one that inspires others.
- You are the star of your own movie.

Chapter 4

Living Life on Your Terms

"Follow your passion; it will lead you to your purpose."

~ Oprah

Many followed the group, instead of their heart. They sought security over purpose, and ended up with neither. These individuals, like so many others, have been programmed from a young age to follow a conventional path. This path was created long ago, to serve a very different time and place, and today it might lead its followers to a very disappointing result. This would be perfectly acceptable if this life were a rehearsal, a test run for the next one, but that's not the case. This is it! This is your one and only life to live as you choose.

So, whether you are just starting out on your journey after graduating college or graduate school, or if you're a mid-career professional trying to ensure that you end up in the right place, then there is good news. Right now, right here, you're where you need to be. This book is your eye-opening journey to a Motivated life.

It's critical before undertaking any new venture, journey, or endeavor, to ask yourself this key question: How do you define success? That is to say, in whatever you're doing, you must begin by knowing your desired outcome. Without this, how can you truly know whether your time and effort was worth the investment?

The desired outcome of this book is for you to create positive change in your life, and to put you on the right path for you. This is referred to herein as a Motivated life. Take note that it's not called a perfect life, because that can only be defined by you. Life is a journey and with any journey, there will always be peaks and valleys. Many of today's inspirational books seem to only focus only on the peaks, and that's not reality. People who live a Motivated life define the terms under which they live. They aren't pursuing an education for security's sake, they don't pick a career for its benefits, and they don't expect life to be easy or without issues. To the contrary, they expect and rejoice in facing the challenges that make them better, that help them grow, and that give them even more confidence for larger obstacles that may arise in the future.

If you're fortunate enough to realize these principles early in life, rather than later, then you are way ahead of the game. The reason why this book begins by placing everyone into two camps, Motivated or Misplaced, is because ultimately, you either feel that you're on the right path and succeeding, or you feel the opposite and know in your heart that it's time for a change. This applies to any area of your life – personal or professional. You want a new path; something that will re-ignite the spark that you had back when all of life's possibilities seemed endless. Remember that feeling when you graduated from high school or college, when you had a feeling that life was merely a blank canvas for you to fill in with whatever you wanted?

The new path that you're about to embark upon comes with a new playbook for your life. If you truly want to change your life and get on the right path for you, you simply cannot maintain your old way of thinking or repeating the same actions from your old playbook. Ask any coach about using the same old playbook year after year, while looking for a winning season. The team becomes predictable and the opponent can easily overtake the predictable team. The players become bored. They get left behind as other teams race past them. After losing game after game, they end up losing hope.

The same old thinking and actions equal the same old life. If you want change, you have to think and act like someone who lives with passion and purpose, not like someone who is drifting along and idly following the crowds or the norms.

Your new path of passion and purpose requires some new strategies. As an example, early on you'll begin by investing in you. Part of investing in yourself is taking the time to create a plan for your life. It also includes reading, studying and learning. Investing in yourself must include having clearly defined and written down life goals.

Jim Rohn, the famous speaker, author and life teacher, talks about the time that his mentor asked him about his goals. At the time, Mr. Rohn was failing miserably in all areas of his life. He was broke, and broken. When Jim's mentor asked to see his list of goals, Jim replied, "I don't have a list." His mentor asked whether that meant that his list was not there with him, or whether he didn't have one at all. Jim answered, "I don't have a list of goals anywhere." With a look of disappointment, his mentor said, "that's a huge mistake and is the first place to start in changing your life." He added that, given the fact that Jim had no goals, he would be able to guess what Jim's bank balance was, within $10,000 dollars. And, he did! Jim asked, "are you suggesting that just by having clearly defined goals that are written down, that my life could change? "Drastically," his mentor said. And it proved to be true.

Goals help you stay enthusiastic about your life rather than merely coast along without having any expectation of reaching any worthwhile destination. Having something to look forward to and achieve is an integral part of living a happy, well-rounded, successful life. Those who find happiness and success in their life are the ones who care enough about themselves to design a new life and adopt new and specific goals that help them move in the direction of their true passion and purpose. Having goals and a plan is crucial to your success. Remember the famous quote by John L. Beckley:

"Most people don't plan to fail, they fail to plan."

In Chapter Nine, you will create your goals and you will have a plan.

So, what will it mean to you to be on your path of passion and purpose? Does it mean that your life will always be easy? Of course not. Does it mean that all your family and friends will support you? You would think so, but no. Does it mean that, suddenly, you'll enjoy every minute of the day? Almost, but no. If you find your path to passion and purpose, you will not be without problems. However, you will have far less fear and you'll be supremely positioned to handle anything that comes your way. You will also reach new levels of joy and energy that you previously thought were only experienced by really successful people. You will also learn to appreciate the following about yourself:

- Why you are here
- What gifts you have
- Your life's ultimate mission
- How to help others reach the same levels of success that you reached

Why is that? It's because true happiness, the type that so few people experience, comes from an inner confidence that comes from growing and advancing, and knowing that no matter what happens to you, you can handle it! Once you've reached this stage, you know in your heart that you've arrived, and that you will never see the world in the same way again. You will also notice that the people around you won't see you the same way either.

There's an inner peace and confidence that comes from knowing that with almost unlimited choices, thousands of possible paths, and a vast array of options, you, and you alone, have made the right choice for your life. You've found a new way, a new path, and it will lead you on an amazing journey. You are living life on your terms – a Motivated life.

Are you ready to invest in yourself? In the famous words of Warren Buffet, the world's greatest investor:

"The most important investment that you can make is in yourself."

Deciding that you will invest in yourself is half the battle. The other half is to keep making the investment and following your plan, even during those times when you doubt yourself or are discouraged by others. You have to adopt a new mindset.

Speaking of mindsets, walking the path of purpose and passion means having the "Entrepreneurial Mindset," by believing that you are in charge of your destiny. It means that you can create the outcome that you want, in order to have the freedom to pursue your dreams and passions.

As an example, let's take a look at the paths that two different people embarked on and where they ended up.

The Story of Matt and Gail

Matt and Gail started out on the same path in life. They both came from good families, were raised well, and were taught to value education. Matt stuck to the traditional, well-traveled conventional path. He soaked up all of the knowledge that he could in school, and took his teachers' words as the gospel. He was a diligent student and, after graduating from high school, borrowed over one hundred thousand dollars to earn a college degree in engineering. He then borrowed even more to earn an MBA. He began his career at 26, working for a large company. By 30, he had been promoted once, and was married with a mortgage. By 35, he had two kids, and was still moving up the ranks. At 45, he was doing quite well as a vice president. He took his job very seriously and sacrificed his personal time along the way, only ever taking off the weekends, holidays, and 1-2 weeks of vacation each year. By

50, Matt was in serious debt. Between the cars, the house, his forever outstanding school loans, private school for the kids, and vacations, he was dependent upon his job to keep things afloat. He couldn't afford to do anything but continue working at his job so that he could bring home the income needed to meet his financial obligations.

When Matt was let go from his company at 51, his whole life was turned upside down. He had spent his entire career building a specific set of skills, which were no longer valuable to his employer. He was at a late stage in his career, and he had to start over. He had to downgrade his lifestyle and take a junior position at another company. He will now work well past retirement age if he can even retire at all. Matt is an example of a Misplaced life.

Gail took a different path. After high school, where she was a solid B student at best, she earned a liberal arts degree at a nearby college. She worked her way through, borrowed no money, and while in college, became interested in building wealth. First, Gail opened an online store specializing in crystals. She made a modest income initially but also learned quite a bit about running a business. By her second year in college, Gail had already invested in stocks and bonds. By her third year, she owned a rental property and had a very solid investment portfolio. Upon graduation, Gail chose to forgo graduate school and instead, spent the next several years building wealth. By 35, Gail was happily married with children, and was a very successful online entrepreneur. She also had three apartment properties, a successful stock portfolio, and a coin collection. By 40, Gail was already a millionaire. At 50, Gail was financially free. As a gift, she paid for her two children's college education so that they could start their adult life without any school debt. Gail is an example of living a Motivated life. She knew what she wanted to do. She knew what a good fit meant for her, and she went after it without wasting any time or money, or creating any regrets.

Matt bought into the old story about taking the traditional path. With few exceptions, that path is based on a fallacy. Worse yet, by the time people like Matt realize it, it's taken over their life and they have to literally restart their careers in their 50s, a time when they should be able to start looking forward to retirement.

On the other hand, while Gail went through the educational system, along the way, she questioned everything she was told and taught. When her high school guidance counselor told her that the only path to success was through a college degree, it did not ring true to her. She could not envision herself sitting through four years of college and working her way up the ranks at a corporation. That way of life did not interest her in the least. Instead, she spent most of her time studying her personal passions and applying those interests to new ventures that helped her learn about building a life on her own terms.

While Matt appeared far more successful during several different stages along the way, it was only a mirage. Matt clung to all of the traditional rules engrained in him by an outdated educational system. Matt was trained to be an employee, to follow directions, to work hard within the box, and to stay on a path that leads to complete reliance on others, like bosses, who usually don't have their employees' best interests in mind. Gail, on the other hand, built the kind of foundation and life that allowed her to have true happiness. This book is about making you think like Gail, no matter what stage of life you're in now.

Most people take a safer path, at least initially. It's one with a wide and comfortable entrance. It feels good since everyone is heading in that same direction, so it must be right. It's not easy, but it's not hard. For the first few years, it seems like the right choice. But before too long, usually at a point when it is too late to turn back, the people on this path realize that they bought a lifestyle, not a life. (And there is a huge difference between a lifestyle and a life!) They also realize that this wrong path will always have them chasing, running, and scrambling just to keep up. In order to stay on this Misplaced path, you will sacrifice your happiness, your identity, and for some, your very own life due to inordinate amounts of stress.

But, it doesn't have to be this way.

The secret to a happy life is not about riches. It's not about status, which is fleeting. It's not about possessions. Ultimately, the true secret of life is about having the freedom and control to live life on your terms, build your dreams, answer to your heart, and not live within the rules of others.

This feeling will come the day that you are truly free, and when you and your family are living by your own rules.

The mission of this book is very simple - to help guide you through the shortest path to freedom from debt, worry, frustration, humiliation, and every other form of entrapment that comes from a life on the conventional path. If you work at it, it will liberate you from living the next twenty years of your life under a cloud of uncertainty, only to find that you have another long road of the same ahead of you.

Motivated Thinking from Chapter 4:	• Conforming to the traditional path will keep you reliant upon others. • Following your own interests puts you on your own path – the one you are meant to be on. • Your passion and purpose will lead you to the ultimate freedom. • Be a Gail, not a Matt.

Part Two: How Did You End Up Here?

~

Chapter 5:

The Conventional Path is An Illusion

"Your time is limited, so don't waste it living someone else's life. Don't be trapped by dogma - which is living with the results of other people's thinking. Don't let the noise of others' opinions drown out your own inner voice. And most important, have the courage to follow your heart and intuition."

~Steve Jobs

What Does the Conventional Path Mean?

You go to school. Study hard. Get good grades. Get into a good college. Borrow money to live while you study. Go to graduate school. Borrow more money. Graduate. Get a job, get a car, get a house. You're $150,000 in debt and beholden to a job, not a dream. You bought a lifestyle, not a life.

That's a brief summary of the conventional path, and it's fooled more people into a false sense of security than any other plan in modern day history. The conventional path is based on the idea of security – and the truth is that you rarely achieve it. Instead, it's always around the next corner, or with the next promotion that never comes. Once you're in debt and have family obligations, you'll do almost anything to maintain a certain level of income and security, even if it means selling yourself out and letting others take advantage of you. And, therein lies the heartbeat of the conventional path – the owners and wealth creators need young, talented people to pursue the conventional path in order to help them create their own Motivated life. That's why it's often said that when you aren't working towards achieving your own goals, you'll end up working towards someone else's.

The Perils of the Conventional Path

In any area of your life, following what most of the other people are doing is almost always a recipe for personal unfulfillment and frustration.

This message is particularly targeted towards young college-aged dreamers who have an ideal opportunity to set up their life the correct way, before the costs, to change course becomes too high. Getting an early start to achieve your Motivated life can only happen through your short-term sacrifice of swimming upstream, against the popular tide, and making your own way in the face of adversity and obstacles presented by those around you.

Every year, thousands of new college and post-college graduates come out of school with a degree and a dream. They've diligently worked their way through a system that rewards passivity, obedience, memorization, and routine. They took on significant debt, spent endless hours studying, and made sacrifices to their personal lives. Starting as early as elementary school, they were told by all around them (family and educators alike) that the conventional path was their only path to success. The mantra has always been that without a college degree, you would never be able to advance in your career, and that you would end up stuck in a low-paying job - one that you hate - for the rest of your life. The strong message taught to everyone, and that is still being taught today, is that one cannot achieve success without first obtaining a traditional college education. Perhaps, without putting too much thought into it, these Misplaced people merely stepped onto that path and remained there, just waiting for that big reward after graduation.

That path is very well-traveled and will continue to be traveled upon for the vast majority of people. Millions of young people travel this path. Get that first job, buy that first house, and work really hard to advance. Save money, invest conservatively, and try to enjoy life during the weekends and yearly vacations. Read that again—enjoy your life during weekends and yearly vacations—less than one-third of your year. Are you supposed to be miserable the other two-thirds or more of each year? Is that what you really signed up for—a life of two relaxing days sandwiched between five days of stress, and a life without purpose and passion? Why would you settle for two days per week of "living," when you can change your life and live a purposeful, meaningful, happy life of gratitude the majority of the year?

Where Does the Road Lead?

It's ten years from now, and you have done what you set out to do. You're an executive with a title, you have a mortgage, a young family, a car loan, college loans, and credit card debt. In terms of the traditional path, the American Dream, you've made it! You have it all. But, are you truly free in the land of the free? How many pay periods could you (and your family) live without a paycheck? How soon would what has taken you years to build crack or crumble if anything were to happen to your job? As you look around when you're on your way to work, do you see many more people just like you? Do they seem free? Is this the life that they envisioned? Is this the life that you dreamed about when you were growing up?

Graduating from college is most definitely a huge accomplishment. You should be proud of yourself for all of the effort that you've extended, and for following through on the commitment you made. Your effort is not in question. The real question is whether you've been on the right path for you. Did you simply step onto the traditional path because that's what you thought you were supposed to do, or because someone else envisioned that for you. What if I told you that, even though you've graduated, if you do not want the scenario described above to become your life, you now need to think differently?

It's not too late to redirect your life. You'll need to unlearn some of what you've learned. And you need to do it fast. If you do not do what this book suggests, you might never be free. With the conventional path, your happiness and success in life will always be tied to the approval of a boss, and the success of a company. It's a tragedy to see professional men and women, late in their careers, beg for acceptance and a paycheck because they placed all of their faith in the traditional path – the path that led to limited options, worry, and entrapment. Have the courage not to take that road. You have the chance now, to take a different path.

Change Your Approach

You've spent many years learning how to think like an employee, developing the mindset and behavior of an employee. Our entire educational system is based on teaching skills that lend themselves to becoming a passive, follow-along, make-no-waves type of person. Just think about Kindergarten, and every grade since then. That was the way your teachers and principals expected you to behave. They engrain a herd mentality into all students because it's easier for educators (and bosses, later on) when every child behaves the same way. How sad! These skills regrettably lead you down the wrong path, and then, as you are straying further away from achieving your Motivated life, a gnawing false sense of comfort makes you feel as though you are actually continuing to advance in your career and in your life. That's because you are still continuing to do all of the wrong things you were told would lead to a successful life. In the words of Jerry Seinfeld:

"Sometimes the road less-traveled is less-traveled for a reason."

The road less-traveled can be rocky and dark at times and may take you through unknown territory. Change and unknown territory can be intimidating. That road forces you to make your own decisions, instead of allowing someone else to make them for you. It forces you to think for yourself and go against the thinking that you've been taught your entire life. There might be risks involved. You might risk hearing your spouse say that you are being foolish or irresponsible or hearing your parents say they are disappointed in you after all they've sacrificed to make sure you could go to college. You might risk losing friends who have traditional goals and aspirations, or you might create strained relationships. The road less-traveled might also include financial risks.

You may fear that once you step off that beaten path, you'll be lost and not even know what step to take next. That traditional path has been your only plan for most of your life—what now? Why bother making changes? Why not continue taking the path of least resistance?

Making decisions and taking calculated risks requires courage. Sure, it's easier if you stay on the beaten path, but the price you might pay for that easier path is your freedom, passion, self-respect, and the probability that you won't attain the life you really want to live. That's an enormous price tag for temporary comfort!

The road-less traveled might not be the easiest road you can take short-term, but it pays off in the long-term. In the short-term, the road less-traveled can be fraught with insecurity. However, keep in mind that there is no guaranteed security on the traditional road. How many times have you heard of men and women in their 50's and 60's getting fired after being loyal to their company for their entire career? If you have a choice between trusting your company or yourself for your future financial security, doesn't it make more sense to trust yourself? After all, you are the only one who totally has your best interests at heart.

If you truly want to move up and succeed in having the life that is right for you, you must change your approach in order to fit that life, rather than trying to make the wrong life fit you! If you try to fit yourself in a box where you don't belong, you will always feel like something is amiss and you will feel uncomfortable. Your heart will always be reminding you that you are Misplaced. You must change your approach rather than continue to think that even though you are Misplaced, everything will still be fine if you would only work harder; just tweak this one thing; just be patient; or just listen to more gurus who preach the same message of conformity and mediocrity.

Working harder isn't the answer. There are only so many hours in the week. It's likely that you already are working as many hours as humanly possible and are probably trying to find every possible angle to please your bosses and colleagues. How could you work harder? And if you could, what would it really accomplish in the end? Would it lead to your happiness?

You can't randomly change one tiny thing and expect your life to change. That is tantamount to thinking that by removing one brick from a building, the entire structure would be dramatically altered. You need to make a lifestyle change. And, while patience truly is a virtue, there are times in your life when patience is used as an excuse due to a fear to move forward.

You can learn great things and gain applicable advice from studying leaders. But none of them, no matter what they say, has a secret or a magic bullet that will automatically change your life for you. YOU are the one who ultimately must apply that information into your life in order for the advice it to be effective. Listening to one more podcast, reading one more book, or attending one more seminar will certainly enhance your life, but it will not change your life unless you take the necessary actions. YOU are the only one who can change your life.

Motivated Thinking from Chapter 5:

- Beware of the well-promoted conventional path.
- Choosing the road less-travelled requires courage and risk-taking.
- The road less-travelled can lead to the life of your choosing.
- To succeed in having the life you want, you must change your approach to life.

Chapter 6:

Traits You Learned That Hold You Back

"Beware of false knowledge; it is more dangerous than ignorance."

~George Bernard Shaw

There is a quote often attributed to Mark Twain that says, "it's not what you don't know that gets you into trouble, it's what you know that just ain't so." Whether he said it or not, it's a brilliant statement. Most books only address what you should know, but few discuss things you already know, that actually might be holding you back. What you've learned has become the framework for how you view the world. And, if your world isn't what you want it to be, it's most likely not the world's fault, but rather how you see it, and operate within it.

You are quite simply the product of what you've learned up until this point of your life. This book is about introducing you to new strategies and concepts, with the goal of producing a new outcome for you. However, this can only happen if you approach the upcoming material with an open mind and a willingness to push yourself to new limits. This will be challenging if your mind has been programmed with certain "Conventional Traits" often promoted in formal education, and encouraged by family members and friends.

Author and Futurist Jay Cross said, "Formal learning is like riding a bus: the driver decides where the bus is going; the passengers are along for the ride. Informal learning is like riding a bike: The rider chooses the destination, the speed, and the route." Which do you think brings the student more freedom?

This chapter is not about the shortfalls of formal education. That's a subject for another time. In order to truly succeed in changing your path in life, you must first recognize that some things that have become part of your daily thinking need to be changed as well. You simply cannot achieve a different output by relying on the same input. Later, you will be led through a series of chapters that will help you change what goes into your mind. For now, it's important to recognize a few traits you might still be adhering to which won't serve you well if you're going to try to achieve a Motivated life.

The Conventional Traits of Formal Education

Most likely, without even knowing it, your formal education and the people closest to you have conditioned you to focus only on knowledge-based learning, and on the environment in which it's promoted. This type of learning has taught you to adhere to some or all of the following "conventional traits." When these traits arise in your thinking, you need to call them out, recognize them for what they are, and challenge them as limiting factors that must be eliminated:

Conventional Trait:	In Practice:
Obedience	Being obedient and listening to authority figures is part of achievement.
Passivity	Learning takes place in a passive environment where the student sits quietly and listens.
Conformity	Conforming to, and following the actions of the group is crucial to success.
Fear of Failure	Failure is a bad thing that should be avoided.
Memorization	Memorizing facts, figures and concepts is a big part of learning.
Target of the Status Quo	The desired outcome is to reach and appreciate the status quo.

Let's briefly look at each of these:

Obedience

Obedience is a great trait for creating followers rather than leaders. Those who gladly obey without questioning what and whom they obey are easily influenced and controlled by others. Obedience conditions people to avoid thinking for themselves, utilizing their natural gifts and talents, and pursuing the path that is right for them. This is an appropriate trait for a robot, but not for a successful human being.

Passivity

In society and in education, there are numerous instances where people are both taught and expected to behave passively. Think about the common classroom scenario where students are taught that when the bell rings, they must find their desk and sit quietly while they await directions. Ironically, the student who is not passive often gets punished for trying to learn in a different way. He or she tries to think outside of the box, and is viewed as disruptive. He or she is often singled out, admonished, and told to quickly return to the group's behavior. Unfortunately, since many companies also adopt this mentality for their employees, the educational system trains students well for that environment.

Conformity

"The biggest challenge of life is to be yourself in a world that is trying to make you like everyone else."

~**Anonymous**

One informal definition of conformity is to remain in compliance with standards, rules, laws, or behavior. Whether you are part of an educational system, organization, work team, family, or social group, you will always be influenced by those around you. You should bear in mind that you always have the ultimate power in deciding whether you will conform to the group's behavior, beliefs, and philosophy. Isn't that the advice that's given to teens during their formative years toward adulthood? Parents tell their teens to exercise their own ability to think for themselves, rather than follow their peers into negative lifestyles. It applies to adults, too. If you develop the mentality that the power to go beyond conformity is yours, and yours alone, you will learn to think for yourself, have the confidence to carry out your own smart ideas, and own what you do. Freedom!

Society has been trained to identify and reject nonconformity. When a person chooses not to conform, they might be ostracized, discriminated against, harassed, or intimidated. They might be viewed as the troublemakers of society, and become devalued and disrespected.

It can be difficult to choose your own path, live by your own values and beliefs, and move away from your own life when you view things differently than others. It's easy to lose your vision, mission, and purpose in life when you lose the sense of who you are. Once your identity is taken away, you lose your sense of excellence. Conformity creates mediocrity.

The Story of Andy

To see how choosing a path other than conformity can be rewarding and lead to a successful career, let's take a look at the career path that Andy took when it was time for him to make serious decisions about his life.

When Andy was sixteen, he spent the summer with his Uncle Greg, who owned a construction company specializing in building environmentally friendly, safe homes suitable for retirees. Andy often visited the job sites with his uncle. Seeing those homes being built sparked an interest in Andy for several reasons. Andy enjoyed working with his hands and working mostly outdoors. He liked utilizing his love for math, in which he excelled. He felt a sense of pride about being a good steward of the environment by creating greener homes. And, he liked the idea of owning and operating his own business.

When Andy returned home and shared his interest in building houses, his parents immediately dissuaded him, doing their best to keep Andy focused on their chosen career path for him, which was becoming a public-school superintendent, like his father. "It's been an excellent career for me," his father said. "You'll enjoy it; the salary and pension will provide well for you; and I can get your feet in the door locally. You'll be a shoe-in for my position by the time you graduate from college, and I'm ready to retire. It's a good, solid plan."

Andy always assumed he would follow the path chosen by his parents. It made sense. He observed that his father was good at his job, and watched him receive many awards and accolades for his service to the school district. Perhaps more important, Andy knew how much it would please his father and mother were he to follow the secure path that had provided so well for their family.

When invited, Andy eagerly accepted his Uncle Greg's invitation to work for his company the following summer. In the three-month period that he worked there, Andy thoroughly enjoyed what he did and felt that he learned more about business math, and applicable math there than he had learned in all of his high school years combined. He was enthusiastic to see how math could actually be applied in real-life situations, on the construction site.

Andy returned home excited about seriously considering the apprenticeship that his uncle offered him once he graduated from high school. However, Andy's parents were upset with Uncle Greg for making the offer, and were even sadder that Andy was considering it. A natural peace-keeper, Andy promised his parents that he would go to college and pursue a career as a school administrator.

After high school graduation, Andy kept his promise to his parents and attended the university closest to his home. He worked hard and kept up his grades. However, he trudged through his first year of college. He didn't experience any excitement or enthusiasm about the prospect of enduring three more years of the same, only to graduate and then sit behind a desk doing administrative work for the rest of his life.

During his first year at the university, on Saturdays and school holidays, Andy journeyed to his Uncle Greg's business. Each time he worked at the construction site, Andy felt alive as he watched his progress on the projects to which he was assigned. He was amazed at how much he learned that could immediately apply in his life —without sitting in a classroom for many hours each week, only to walk away with the feeling that he learned little to nothing of relevance to his own life. The more time he spent working in his uncle's business, the more Andy knew that he was making a mistake by not accepting his uncle's offer for an apprenticeship.

Meanwhile, and through no fault of his own, with only three years left to retirement from a job where he had an exemplary record of service, Andy's father lost his job as school superintendent due to a quickly-changing political environment. While Andy felt terrible for his father, he used the incident as a vehicle to get his father's blessing to leave school and accept the apprenticeship.

With his father's blessing, Andy left the university. He quickly signed up for a business class and a marketing class at the local community college. He purchased an online course that, upon passing the state-required tests, would meet the state licensing requirements for a contractor's license. For the next year, Andy learned both the business side and craft side of the green-building industry.

By the time he was 23 years old, Andy owned his own green construction company that he thoroughly enjoyed operating. He didn't have any student loans. He didn't dread going to work. He looked forward to implementing his new ideas and continuing to learn all that he could to expand and grow his business. He was not locked into a nine-to-five (or later) daily work routine dictated by someone else. This freedom in making his own work schedule came in very handy a few years later when he and "Mrs. Andy" welcomed their first child into their happy, prosperous world.

As you can see, Andy is a great example showing how being Motivated or Misplaced can make such a huge difference in your life. If conforming to someone else's plan for your career path is Misplacing you, it's time to say goodbye to that type of conformity. It's time to respectfully bow out of someone else's dream for your life, and start living your own dream life.

Fear of Failure

> **"Too many of us are not living our dreams, because we're living our fears."**
>
> **~Les Brown**

Failure is a necessary part of success. However, many of us have been conditioned to view failure as a negative experience that should be avoided at all costs. Fear of failure sets boundaries in many people's lives that they can never break through. Instead, they live within these pre-conceived notions, and end up becoming risk-adverse. There's a story that's often told about the way trainers teach a young elephant to avoid escaping. They tie it to a metal stake in the ground and put it on a very short rope. At first, the young elephant tries to roam in order to escape. However, it's not strong enough to break the rope. The young elephant's boundaries end up being defined for him. After that point, the rope and the stake can be removed with the elephant staying within the same area because it's been conditioned that it simply can't go any further. Ironically, people can be trained the same way. We start out in life not knowing what we cannot do, but along the way, there are plenty of people and teachers that help us establish our limits. Once we have them, we live within them.

You simply cannot go after your dreams and create a new life for yourself if you fear failure. Instead, you need to view failure as an indication that you are trying things, and that one way or another, after enough failures, you will find your way to success!

Memorization

Memorization only teaches people that they have to believe what they are told, simply because the information was provided to them from a person with authority—namely teachers and supervisors. Under this paradigm, students and workers are conditioned that the information, the methods of teaching, and the paths they are taught are not to be questioned. Worse yet, students and workers automatically believe that the information they are taught must be true, accurate, and followed.

Memorization imitates education. A person who is taught memorization can recite what they have memorized without understanding what they are reciting. As an example, a high school student may memorize historical dates in order to ace a history test, but he probably has no idea of how the events which happened on that date changed people's lives, or the significance that it had in the world. What good is the recitation of facts when there is no understanding of how that information can be applied in a person's personal or professional life? Is your end goal to simply have a brain filled with memorized facts? No, of course not. Your goal is to retain information that you can utilize in your real life to meet your personal goals.

The media often repeats certain headlines or statements over and over until the public memorizes what they hear and accepts it as fact, even when the statements are not facts at all. This is the reason why most adults merely accept what they read or hear in the media, without any questioning whatsoever. They have been brainwashed to merely accept what is told to them rather than think about what they are told and determine for themselves whether or not it is true. Since they are learning "facts" from people with authority, they wrongly assume that the "facts" must be true. It's very sad but quite understandable how this has happened. It's simply the result of years of being told what to learn, memorize, and accept, from people of "authority," without questioning them.

It's tantamount to the messaging of dictators and fascists. They repeat the same untrue statements and ideologies to people who merely accept the horrific message rather than think for themselves. This can yield many very scary and horrific results. Just look at World War II.

Status Quo

Status quo is the existing state of affairs, especially regarding social or political issues. The status quo and the demand to maintain it is an illusion to avoid change. When maintaining the status quo causes a detriment to the productivity and well-being of society, you must open your mind and ask yourself why you are being taught to maintain the status quo. The answer might very well be a fear of change or progress, regardless of the dysfunction of the current system.

Status quo can easily, yet mistakenly appear as an extension of democracy, especially when its advocates claim that everyone agrees, regardless of the facts or the recognition of its inherent corruption. This is constantly playing out in the media, in our educational institutions, and in our government, and it's pathetic.

George Orwell's 1984 provides a clear illustration of what happens when the goal is to simply maintain the status quo. The novel also highlights many other traits that have been learned, which actually must be unlearned if a person truly cherishes the freedom to be who they are and walk their own path of success.

Why These Conventional Truths and Traits Lead to a Misplaced life

After thinking about your own "Conventional Traits," and recognizing the influence they may have had in your life, here's an interesting experiment for you. Hold that list up to your computer screen while you use Google to pull up a picture of a truly successful person (use your own definition of a successful person). Look at the image of the successful person, then look at these "Conventional Traits." How many of the traits do these highly-successful people possess? How many of these traditional traits do you see in a star athlete, successful business owner, CEO, or talented leader and influencer? I'm fairly certain that the answer is none. Does it ever occur to anyone that the "Conventional Traits" can be found in your average robot?

As you reflect upon your life, keep this in mind: The "Conventional Traits" were not traits and skills taught to instill freedom of choice in your life, so that you could pursue their dreams. These traits were not created to provide options. Rather, these traits were fostered to create a passive, obedient, standardized, easily-controlled classroom, workforce, and society. You no longer choose to participate in this paradigm.

A Word about Formal Education

In recent history, there has been much discussion about school reform. In actuality, schools, including the best Ivy League schools, most likely fear any type of reformation because they are functioning in a manner that accomplishes their intended purpose. If your purpose for your life is different from their purpose for your life, it's your responsibility to pursue your purpose and to find your own success and happiness. While most people will continue to advocate for you to take the well-trodden path, you must remember that you have options.

As John Taylor Gatto, author and award-winning New York City public school system teacher for over 30 years put it, "You either learn your way towards writing your own script in life or you unwittingly become an actor in someone else's script."

Motivated Thinking from Chapter 6:

- The educational system, along with your family and friends, taught you Conventional Traits that hold you back.
- Unlearning these traits can be just as important, or even more important, than learning new traits and strategies.
- A Motivated life requires new thinking, as well as eliminating old thinking.
- What else have you learned, that you should now unlearn?

Chapter 7:

Traits That You Should Have Learned

"Learning is a Treasure that Will Follow its Owner Everywhere."

~Chinese Proverb

Learning something new can literally change your life! In the previous chapter, we highlighted that certain Conventional Traits, if engrained in your thinking, need to be eliminated. Conversely, there are other traits that will help propel you to the life that you want. Some of the more prevalent are the focus of this chapter.

Contrary to what you may have been taught, you can choose to think and act on your own. Through self-development, you can become influential, creative, self-aware, competitive, and untraditional—all traits that you should have learned and now, must learn.

Those who are successful and have the freedom to live their lives on their own terms, know that they must act instead of react to life. They understand that they must be on the offensive instead of the defensive. They understand that they can't wait around to see where someone wants them to go, but must decide for themselves where to go and start taking the steps to get there.

Those who find success know they can't wait for the perfect timing until all their ducks are in a row, or until they feel motivated by outside sources. In fact, they understand the truth that author Paul J. Meyer states in this quote, "No matter who you are or what your age may be, if you want to achieve permanent, sustaining success, the motivation that will drive you toward that goal must come from within."

The Success Traits that You Must Learn on Your Own:

There are various traits that are part of any successful person. They're on display every day, and scores of books have been written about them. They're highlighted here as a pre-cursor to your journey ahead. The following is but a brief list of some of the top traits that you must deploy if you're going to advance your life.

These "Success Traits" are proactive traits that you must make part of your daily life from now on. They include:

SUCCESS TRAIT: IN PRACTICE:

INFLUENCE	The ability to influence others is a core tenet of success.
CREATIVITY	Being creative separates you from the group and makes you unique.
COMPETITIVENESS	Winning matters, and the desire to win is a foundation of the Motivated life.
UNCONVENTIONAL THINKING	Avoiding group think is pivotal.
SELF-AWARENESS	Learning what makes you do what you do is critical to your future success.
STRESS MANAGEMENT	Managing stress is a winning trait that many never seem to master.
ESTABLISHING LIFE GOALS	Goals are paramount to achieving the life that you want.
MANAGING YOUR OWN FINANCIAL PLAN	Planning for your financial peace of mind is an absolute requirement, and is much easier than it sounds.

Now, take the same picture that you looked at on Google as instructed in the previous chapter, and hold it up again. Does the successful person you selected possess these five traits? Does the person influence others? Does he/she find creative solutions to problems? Are they self-aware and know their own strengths and weaknesses (that is, when to lead and when to rely on others)? Is the person competitive? And finally, is it a person who follows the crowd, or one who behaves uniquely and untraditional in their approach, bringing something fresh and valuable to the world?

People are not simply born successful. Those who create a successful life have learned the traits that are conducive to success. Below is a more in-depth look into these traits that will help lead you to achieve a Motivated life.

Influence

The ability to influence others is key to your future success. What is an influencer? There are many definitions for the word influencer. Simply put, an influencer is one who has the power to affect the behavior and decisions of others. In marketing, the influencer is the person who uses their persuasive writing or sales pitch to cause people to take an intended action, such signing up for something or purchasing a service or product. You may have heard people say that their high school/college basketball coach or teacher has influenced them. Obviously, influencers can influence people in positive or negative ways. In this book, the influencer is referred to as one who impacts people's lives in a positive manner and creates positive change wherever they go, and in whatever they do.

Rather than being influenced by other people, you can become the influencer and leader in your relationships, home, workplace, organizations, and society. Influencers can make a positive difference because he or she can make things happen. They can get things done when others can't. They can be culture-changers. Have you ever watched an organization change for the better seemingly overnight when an abusive leader was booted, and then replaced with a compassionate one? And what a difference an influencer can make in the politics of a state or nation! From serving on your local school board to serving as CEO of a major corporation, to successfully starting and operating your own business, you can be an influencer.

Influencers Have a Vision

Influencers understand the vision, and they make sure that the vision is clear to them and to those they are trying to lead. Theodore Hesburgh said, "The very essence of leadership is that you have a vision. It's got to be a vision you can articulate clearly and forcefully on every occasion. You can't blow an uncertain trumpet." Influencers understand this clearly and they use it to their advantage.

Brainstorm your vision and become clear on exactly what it is that you want to accomplish – your desired outcome. If your vision is clear to you, you should be able to state it in just a few concise sentences. Many leaders find it helpful to think and write about their vision every few days or even weekly. It keeps the vision clear and alive in their mind, and also allows them to realize when or if they are expending time, energy, and resources on things that don't line up with their desired outcome. This exercise is extremely helpful for staying on track, which is critically important if you're going to make progress.

Influencers Build Genuine Relationships

Influencers gain the trust of others by developing genuine relationships. To develop these relationships, the influencer must be a sincere person with pure motives. This means no playing games, no manipulation, and no dishonesty. You must truly desire to build a relationship that works for both parties, both teams, or both organizations.

Successful leaders get to know the people they hope to influence. The influencer doesn't simply gather facts about people. Rather, they learn what those people think about, what they believe, and what they need. In his book, "Millionaire Success Habits," Dean Graziosi talks about the concept of how people are influenced by those influencers who have demonstrated that they understand them. People very much want to be understood rather than "sold" on something.

Relationship-building takes time. It doesn't happen in a fast moment. Rather, it's a long-term process of demonstrating your trustworthiness, dependability, and sincerity. If you want to be an influencer, you must invest time in building relationships.

Here are Some Additional Traits of Influencers:
- **Show appreciation for others**. Whatever influencers accomplish, it's because of the help, support, and inspiration from other people. Influencers give credit

where credit is due. They show their appreciation at every given opportunity.
- **Act responsibly.** When influencers take on something, they see it through to the end. When they commit to something, they stand behind it. When they don't feel like doing something that is their responsibility, they do it anyway.
- **Listen to others' perspectives**. Influencers are never so myopic that they only see their own perspective. They realize that fresh perspectives can help solve problems and help others move forward and innovate.
- **Live a life of integrity, even when it seems no one else is looking.** You can't teach one way of life to your team and live another way in your own life, without losing their respect. Influencers have integrity and can be trusted.
- **Manage their emotions**. Everyone has bad days, but an influencer manages their emotions through any type of day. Volatile leaders who explode in anger at the drop of a hat are rarely trusted. Influencers learn to balance professionalism and sincerity with logic which ensures that those around them know what they can expect.
- **Inspire others**. Influencers live life in such a way that those around them are inspired to improve their own lives. This doesn't mean that they're perfect, just that they continually strive to be better each day.
- **Maintain priorities**. Even during tough times. Influencers set a foundation for consistency and maintain their priorities no matter what happens.
- **Give credit where credit is due**. Influencers don't take credit for others' ideas or work. If they borrow from someone, they give them credit. If someone helped them, they give them credit.
- **Help others grow without fear of being surpassed.** Some leaders keep all of their "secrets for success" to themselves because they fear that their success might be diminished, or that they will be surpassed if they help others. The fact is, the more you help others, the more successful you'll become.
- **Do not undermine others**. The high road to success is not achieved by stomping on the heads of others. Influencers find a way to cooperate with, and not undermine the efforts of others, rather than undermining their efforts, even when the opportunity to do so presents itself.

- **Responsive to the needs of others**. As a leader, influencers are often called upon for help. They try to be responsive to the needs of others. They listen to their needs and see whether they can help them achieve their desired outcome.
- **Improve their skill sets as needed**. Influencers realize that no one ever truly "arrives." Constant learning is a key to success!

Creativity

> "Creativity is the way that I share my soul with the world."
>
> ~Brene Brown

Creative thinking allows you to look at situations and topics in different ways. When you open up your mind to creative thinking, you also open it up to new possibilities. Allowing yourself to have an open mind will give you the clarity to positively view any situation. With creativity, you can also find ways to solve everyday problems in the most efficient way. Creative thinking will also give you the ability to present and interpret topics and information in fun, or interesting ways.

We are all born creative, but somewhere along the way, we stifle this important trait. Try a new adventure that exposes you to new physical and mental views, thoughts, and perspectives. Try new things that challenge you. It's too easy to become buried in your work and forget that you have a brain that needs refreshment. Don't let that happen!

Competitiveness

To succeed, you must be competitive. To be competitive, you must develop certain skills. You probably already possess some of these skills. Some of the skills might come naturally to you, while you might have to learn and develop others. While a study of each skill is beyond the scope of this book, don't worry! All of these skills can be learned by reading books, taking online classes or classes at community college, attending seminars, and working with a mentor or coach. The main thing is to have a willingness to learn and practice the skills, and to set aside the time to do so.

Here is a List of Skills to Develop in order To Be a Competitive Leader:

- **Verbal and Oral Communication Skills**. Excellent verbal and oral communication skills allow you to clearly express your ideas, thoughts, vision, and instructions in a clear, concise, and professional manner. As an influencer, you will use communication skills constantly. Developing communication skills should be a priority for any influencer.
- **Negotiation Skills**. Negotiation skills must be learned if you expect to achieve your interests in any situation. Learning from a coach or mentor who has mastered negotiation skills is one of the best ways to becoming a great negotiator. If you have a colleague who is known for their negotiation skills, invite them to lunch and ask if they're willing to provide an overview of their thinking and actions when negotiating.
- **Time Management and Organizational Skills**. There will never be enough time to accomplish everything that you want to accomplish, but every person has the exact same number of hours in their day. The difference between achievers and underachievers is how they use those hours. If you can manage your hours in a way that serves you well in accomplishing your goals, then you will be far ahead of the game. Time management allows you to retain control of your day, week, month, life. Use it for the beneficial tool that it can be.
- **Team-Building Skills**. Create and managing a quality, cooperative team that is cohesive and capable of following through to achieve optimal results, is an outstanding skill. Building a solid team tests the skills of any successful leader. This includes leading team members to work together for the common good and desired outcome. An influencer knows how to motivate and encourage team members, as well as support them.
- **Problem-Solving Skills**. Problems are in essence, opportunities. The leader can either focus on the problem or they can focus on the solution. Focusing on the solution is positive and productive, and keeps all efforts on the desired outcome.

Here are a few tactics used in developing problem-solving skills:

> ✓ *Clearly define the problem.* Sounds simple, right? Too often, what seems to be the problem is just a symptom of the problem. Dig deeper and make sure you've found the root of the issue.

- ✓ *Brainstorm possible solutions.* Once the problem has been identified, create a list of possible solutions, ranking them by time to completion. Include others in the brainstorming process. Listen to other ideas. Remain open-minded and let your solution ideas flow freely.

- ✓ *Establish the steps that must be taken to execute the solution.* Share the steps with those involved in the solution and create your plan of action.

• **Decision-Making Skills**—Leaders take responsibility for making tough decisions. First and foremost, they make decisions and move forward because they know that not making a decision is a bad decision.

Here are some tips for helping you make good decisions:

- ✓ *Take action.* While you'll want to give plenty of thought to the decision, don't put it off for the sake of not having to deal with it. Once you are presented with the need to make a decision, make the decision before not making it becomes a problem.

- ✓ *Seek help from a mentor.* Asking for guidance from a mentor can be one of the best decisions you make!

- ✓ *View the decision from a practical and logical perspective rather than an emotional one.* Emotional decisions can often backfire. Stick to logic and facts.

- ✓ *Consider how the decision you make will affect everyone involved.* Only a few decisions will turn out to be a win-win for everyone, but you should attempt to make decisions that bring value to all involved.

- ✓ *When you realize that you've made a bad decision, admit it, and try to correct it as soon as possible.* Take responsibility for the decision and deal with the fallout like a true professional.

Unconventional Thinking

Successful leaders are unconventional thinkers. They inspire their teams to do amazing things. Under their leadership, bold visions and big feats become a reality. The more challenges facing a company is facing, the greater the need for unconventional thinkers.

Unconventional thinkers create organizations focused on innovation and risk-taking that redefine their markets and sometimes, even the way that people live. Unconventional thinkers beat the competition on a regular basis because they redefine the market in a way where they are in front.

Ironically, the people with the most education and experience are often the most conventional thinkers. Think for a moment about Steve Jobs and Mark Zuckerberg. Both are prime examples of unconventional thinkers and leaders. Their backgrounds are contrary to what most people would expect from a successful corporate leader. They both dropped out of college early and have no formal management experience. Despite this, or maybe because of this, they have led the creation of very unconventional, successful companies.

Unconventional leaders are unconventional thinkers who stand out compared to most people. Their ideas are often counter-intuitive to traditional ideas. They often rely on very simple concepts to create new solutions to new or old problems. Their unparalleled thinking is often reflected in their unique mix of interests and people with whom they associate. They enjoy a wide array of information and ideas, and often focus on things that most people would easily overlook. Unconventional people like to think differently. To illustrate this point, below is a comparison between conventional and unconventional thinkers.

Conventional Thinkers

Conventional thinkers tend to have the following traits:

- They seek safety.
- They avoid risk.
- They are often heard saying things like, "This is just the way we do things" and "Everyone does it this way."
- They accept things as they are.
- They avoid expressing their ideas unless there's a consensus.

- They follow the crowds because there's safety in numbers.
- They believe that group agreement is very important.
- They have a negative perception of things that are very different.
- They don't question why things are the way they are.

Unconventional Thinkers

Unconventional thinkers tend to have the following traits:

- They have a constant quest for perfection.
- They think and act differently from others.
- They constantly question beliefs & assumptions, and make changes when necessary.
- They do not care what other people think.
- They like change, and see it as an opportunity for improvement.
- They are willing to try new things & learn from them.
- They believe that conflict is good because it leads to new ideas and a better outcome.
- They openly express their thinking.
- They value creative thinking.

Although it might not be easy to change and adopt these traits, conventional thinkers can become more unconventional in time. We are actually all born unconventional thinkers. Unfortunately, as we get older, we are taught to think like everyone else and ultimately become conventional thinkers.

"Everyone is born a genius, but the process of living de-geniuses them."

~R. Buckminster Fuller

The takeaway here is that, since conventional thinking can be learned, it can also be unlearned. You might not become as unconventional as Steve Jobs, but you can become far more unconventional than you are now. Below are some ideas that will help:

Become a More Unconventional Thinker

- Always try new things.
- Question everything that you believe.
- Stop doing something just because it's what everyone else is doing.
- Be comfortable when people don't agree with you.

- Always express your thoughts, even if others don't agree with you.
- Converse with people with whom you disagree in order to understand their point of view.
- Accept different ideas.
- Learn from people who are totally different from you.
- Try new ideas even if you have no idea whether they will work.
- View failure as part of the learning required to try new things and as part of the cost of creativity and innovation.
- Use humor and don't be afraid to make fun of yourself when things don't work out.

Self-Awareness

In his best-selling book **"Emotional Intelligence,"** Psychologist Daniel Goleman defines self-awareness as "knowing one's internal states, preference, resources and intuitions." Essentially, this means that we have the ability to monitor our inner world, our thoughts and emotions. Self-awareness doesn't only concern the things we notice about ourselves.

Our mind is very good at storing information on how to react to a certain event. This information forms a blueprint of our emotional life over time, and ends up conditioning our mind to respond in a defined way when we have a similar event in the future. Self-awareness allows us to recognize and understand these preconceptions and in the process, gives us the ability to change it.

Why is Self-Awareness Important?

Self-awareness is the key to emotional intelligence, according to Daniel Goleman. The ability to monitor our emotions and thoughts from moment to moment is key to understanding ourselves better, being at peace with who we are, and proactively managing our thoughts, emotions, and behaviors.

In addition, self-aware people tend to act consciously rather than react passively, are in good psychological health, and have a positive outlook on life. They also have greater depth-life experience and are more likely to show more compassion toward themselves and others.

A number of researchers have identified the trait of self-awareness as a crucial trait of successful business leaders. Green Peak Partners and Cornell University examined 72 executives at public and private companies with revenues from $50 million to $5 billion. Their study found that "a high self-awareness score was the strongest predictor of overall success."

Self-awareness is "arguably the most fundamental issue in psychology, from both a developmental and an evolutionary perspective," and is indeed a complex subject. Perhaps it is the journey of exploring, understanding and becoming ourselves that makes life worth living.

Stress-Management

Stress saps creativity. Do you constantly feel stressed? It doesn't have to be that way. For one thing, you can make changes in your life that will diminish the stress that society relentlessly tries to put on your shoulders.

Here are some practical stress-management techniques to help alleviate the symptoms of stress:

- ✓ *Set your own expectations for yourself rather than letting others create expectations for you.*

- ✓ *Take control of your schedule as much as possible so that you don't feel overwhelmed.* Being busy and being productive are not the same thing. Learn the difference and choose productivity over busyness.

- ✓ *Learn to say no to certain activities that are not meaningful or don't line up with your goals.* There are always a million great things that you could be doing. That doesn't mean you should do them, especially when doing them causes stress in your life. Prioritize, and stay focused on your goals.

- ✓ *Remember, it's about the journey more than the destination.* Don't demand perfection from yourself. Commit to doing your very best and remaining steadfast and productive. Commit to self-development and moving forward but drop the desire for perfection or you'll always be stressed and disappointed. Perfection is not achievable and trying to achieve perfection is extremely stressful. Constantly striving to improve and make progress is the key!

✓ *Exercise daily, even if it's just walking for a few blocks. Exercise is a wonderful stress-reliever.*

Establishing Life-Changing Goals and Managing Your Own Financial Plan

These two subjects must be mentioned here, but because they integral to your future Motivated life, there are entire chapters dedicated to each later in the book. Get ready!

Motivated Thinking from Chapter 7:

- Successful people use a set of key traits to help propel them to their desired outcome.
- Being able to influence others is a core tenet of your future success. Influencers have unique traits that must be learned.
- Thinking creatively sets you apart from others.
- Winning matters! Being competitive is key.
- Avoid "groupthink" by becoming an unconventional thinker.
- Being self-aware helps you understand why you do what you do.
- Managing stress is a very important trait that many never master.
- Learning to set life-changing goals is transformational.
- Learning to manage your own financial plan is critical to your future success.
- What more do you need to learn to become successful?

Part Three: 8 Steps to Help You Create the Life That You Want!

Overview

You are about to make a shift. Up until this point, you've been asked to think about your life today, and to think about what is needed when creating change. Now, the focus will be on the specific tactics that you will use to drive change. The following strategies, in one form or another, have been used by successful people for generations. As you read about the following eight steps, it's critical that you stop and remind yourself to think differently from you have in the past. The mindset you have developed affects every choice you make. Your life is made up of the choices you make. If you've been living a Misplaced life, you've been making choices that led you there and kept you there. If you want to live a Motivated life, you must develop a mindset that causes you to make the kind of choices that lead to a Motivated life. It definitely will be challenging at times, but it is not a standard that is out of reach for you.

You can do this!

You cannot remain where you are merely comfortable. Being comfortable is not your goal. Comfort might be enticing and appealing to you for the short-term, but it will not deliver the results you want. Yielding to comfort instead of moving forward to satisfy that longing in your heart for a better life, can keep you stuck without choices and freedom. You must set aside temporary comfort and stretch yourself to focus on your future growth. Each of the steps in this book were designed to help you do just that. The strategies are explained in broad detail, and then specific action steps are given to help you succeed.

So, what does it mean to live life on a new level? It means that you must immerse yourself in new habits, rituals, and a new focus on how to produce successful results—the results you want. You can do it! And you will, one step at a time.

Later in the book, when you set your goals, you will begin to vividly see how even the smallest daily change can produce huge results for you long-term. Although small changes are easy to make, don't underestimate the power of a small change. The small changes that you make in your life will lead to larger changes for a truly changed life—a Motivated life! How do you do it? Read on. It's simpler than you think.

Chapter 8:

Step 1

Visualize That it's Yours!

"To bring anything into your life, imagine that it's already there."

~ Richard Bach

Jim Carrey, the famous actor and comedian Jim Carrey tells a story about how when he was a broke and struggling comedian, he would quite often visualize things going his way. He had a special location that he would visit each day where he would visualize the future he wanted. Instead of seeing himself as a struggling and rejected entertainer, as was true in his real life, he imagined himself as being wildly successful. He visualized people who had previously rejected him saying yes to him, and pictured other famous people embracing his talent. He envisioned himself involved in large productions, and actively sought after by the elite. This culminated with Jim actually writing an $10M dollar check to himself, which he dated three years into the future. As it turned out, only a few months before that check came due, he was offered $10M to star in "Dumb and Dumber."

This is but one example of the power of visualization. Gifted athletes use it, successful businesspeople rely on it, and people from all walks of life have used it for years to clearly see something in their mind before they then create it in the physical world.

Your mind is powerful. If used properly, it can be a valuable asset in helping you achieve the life that you want. Training your mind for success is not difficult to do but does require that you take intentional actions. Since your mind can be trained both consciously and subconsciously, when you do not train it for success, it might just as easily be trained for the opposite.

Do you ever take the time to see the life that you want in your mind? I mean to really visualize it, and see it as if it's your reality. That's what visualization is all about. Long before the life that you want becomes your reality, you need to begin seeing it and living it in your mind.

If you can train yourself to create the life that you want in your mind, and to often vividly see and feel it, the universe will begin to work with you to make it your reality.

> **"You must be the person you have never had the courage to be. Gradually, you will discover that you are the person, but until you can see this clearly, you must pretend and invent."**
>
> **~ Paul Coelho**

Visualization Helps You Train Your Mind to Expect Success

Before you can believe in anything, you must see it first, and then believe that it's worth achieving. In other words, you must grasp a mental image of what you want to feel or achieve. Visualizing the life and circumstances that you want is a simple but powerful technique to manifest those things in your life. When you visualize your desired outcome, you begin to see it as something that is possible to obtain, and it trains your mind to focus on achieving it. Your mind wants to accommodate your goals and dreams. It is wired for your success!

Visualization might be a totally new concept for you; one that you've never heard of or explored. You might be wondering how it can help in the business arena or help in changing your life from Misplaced to Motivated. Visualization is real, and it works. It's a completely developed and tested method of performance improvement supported by scientific research. It's been used by many successful athletes and business leaders, as well as in the medical field for health and healing. Studies have shown that athletes have successfully used visualization to increase performance, drive motivation, improve skills, and decrease fear. Star athletes like Michael Jordan, Larry Bird, Tiger Woods, and many others have all spoken publicly about how they visualize their success first in their mind, long before they see the results in their arena. You don't have to be a star athlete to use this powerful technique. It works for anyone who invests the time to make it work.

How do you begin? Start each day by taking a few minutes to see yourself in your mind, the way that you want to be. Don't paint a vague picture with broad strokes. Use a small brush to create details in your picture. Focus on the specifics of what you want your life to look like. All change begins from within, and if you can do that, the outer action steps will be much easier.

Two Ways to Use Visualization

There are two ways to effectively use visualization. Later in this book, you will set some short-term and immediate-term goals that lead to the outcomes you want to see in your life. Visualization plays a key role because it helps you see the outcome, and the reward, if you will, for the tenacity and effort that you will put forth to reach your desired results. This is outcome visualization and is very powerful. It's best to practice outcome visualization at night before you go to sleep so that it stays in your subconscious mind. When you wake up the next morning, the sweet feeling of having achieved your goal might still be fresh in your mind so that you "feel" the vision happening.

Outcome Visualization: See the End Result as If You're Living Them

As an example of Outcome Visualization, consider this scenario: Your goal is to get a promotion at work, so you visualize yourself sitting in your new office. Take in the details as though you are watching a movie where the camera has slowly panned around the office for the viewer. See your name plate with the title under it, on the door as you enter the office. Nice! You've always wanted to see that!

Now, see the executive desk that is so much more spacious than the one in your previous small cubicle workspace. Notice the window facing the desk allowing the sunshine to stream in, providing a view of the magnificent skyline. Let your eyes rest on that comfortable executive chair that has replaced your task chair –you know the one—it's the chair that sent you home each day with a lower-back ache. Imagine the comfort of that new chair.

Now, you've stepped into your office. What does it feel like to be in your new office? Does it make you proud to know how hard you have worked and that you have accomplished your goal? Imagine your colleagues, significant other, friends, and family shaking your hand and congratulating you on your promotion. Doesn't that feel good? Doesn't it cause gratitude swelling up within you then you imagine your wonderful accomplishment? Hold on to those feelings!

Envision what you will do and how you will perform in your new job. Who will seek you out for help? How will you help them? How will you lead your colleagues differently in your new position? How can you impact the changes you believe will benefit everyone in the organization? This is outcome-based visualization.

Tactics Visualization: See Yourself Taking the Steps to Attainment

The second form of visualization is Tactics Visualization. This type of visualization focuses on seeing yourself take each necessary action step to reach the desired outcome. As an example, if your goal is to become physically fit and healthy, you could see yourself getting up every morning and walking, going to the gym on your lunch break, and eating superfoods that enhance physical health. You could visualize each detail of these steps to train your mind for success in becoming physically fit and healthy.

If your goal is to give a keynote speech at a gala for a charity that you whole-heartedly support in every way, you can imagine yourself reading articles and books on how to give a good speech; pinpointing what you want to address; jotting down notes you want to include in the speech; writing the speech; and going to a Toastmasters International meeting to practice giving the speech and gaining tips and advice from fellow members. As you visualize these steps, it's easy for your mind to organically go to each step and accomplish them. The outcome is a heart-felt speech that influences your audience members to reach for their checkbooks and write big checks for your charity.

Perhaps your goal is to have a better relationship with your significant other. You can visualize re-arranging your schedule and calendar to spend more time with them; communicating more frequently and in a way that doesn't insult, patronize, or isolate; changing your poor habits that are sabotaging the relationship; and finding ways to make your significant other a true priority in your life. As you visualize these steps, your mind becomes conditioned to practicing each step. The end result is an improved, deeper relationship with your significant other.

As you've seen, this type of visualization is action-based. Envisioning the action steps that lead to the accomplishment of your goal is motivating and empowering. Visualization for the purpose of changing your life is a powerful tool, but, like all good tools, needs to be applied consistently to make consistent progress. Let visualization become a part of your daily life. Here are some steps to help:

Create a Vision Board

A vision board is a collection of images that reflect your dreams and aspirations. Creating a vision board is a great way to help you start imagining and seeing what you want to materialize in your life.

Here are some helpful steps to create a vision board:

- **Determine what you want to achieve in your life— a goal, a feeling, a habit, a possession, a relationship—whatever is important to you.**
- **Select pictures, images, words, symbols, poems, inspirational quotes, and affirmations, etc. that represent what you want to achieve.** For example, if your goal is to increase your monthly income, your symbols might include things that come from that increase – a new home, an exotica vacation, or a new car. Vision boards are unique to the person creating them. There is no right or wrong in choosing your symbols to achieve your goal.
- **Select a board of your preferred type.** Some use poster boards, while others use actual boards. It doesn't matter! The important thing is to make it a physical presence in your life and to make it yours.
- **Attach the things that you chose to represent what you want to achieve onto your board.** Rather than putting everything on one board and complicating something that should be simple, consider creating several boards, perhaps one for each goal, or one for each area of your life: personal, finances, career, family, spiritual, and health, *etc.*
- **Your board should be simple and clear.** Keep it simple so that your goals and messages to yourself are clear and don't get lost amidst the clutter of a complicated board.

- **Place your board out in the open in your living space, where you will see it frequently.** Let what you see inspire you, evoke emotions, encourage you to move forward, create a desire for accomplishment, and create gratitude for all that you are changing and accomplishing in your life.

Be Very Specific in Your Use of Visualization

- **When you visualize, visualize the entire scenario, not just the beginning or ending of what you want to see happen.** All the steps and happenings between the beginning and ending are also important to the process.
- **When you visualize, don't allow your mind to try to figure out how to make what you visualize happen.** If you get bogged down with how you can make things happen, you're actually leaving the realm of visualization and entering the realm of problem-solving. Visualization is not a problem-solving process, though, at times, after a visualizing session, you might find that solutions actually come to you. While visualizing, simply enjoy the scene of your desired outcome and savor the feelings that come along with it: victory, peace, joy, accomplishment, etc.
- **Pay close attention to the details**. The details make your scenario real for you.

By having the courage to visualize what you want your life to be like, and framing your mindset for the Motivated life, you begin to move your life forward even if in reality you appear to be the same person.

Motivated Thinking from Chapter 8:	- To change your life, you must change your mindset. What you think is what you do. - Visualization is a powerful tool that will help you achieve the changes you want in your life. - Using specific visualization techniques will help you stay focused on achieving your Motivated life.

Chapter 9

Step 2

Invest in Yourself

"The only person that you're destined to become is the person that you decide to be."

~Ralph Waldo Emerson

There is no better investment that you can make than investing in yourself. Before you grow your life, expand into new areas, and create a plan with goals, you need to make a conscious decision that you will invest in yourself. Most people who refuse to take the time and effort to invest in themselves end up burned out, without reaching their goals.

You are the CEO of you. You're in charge, and since you're in charge, more opportunities than you can imagine are available to you! You can take this leadership position and do whatever you want with it. However, in order to succeed in that powerful position, you must have the constant physical, mental, and emotional energy, commitment, and vision to follow through. Without those, you won't have the passion required to drive your goals home. Instead, you'll succumb to the daily routine of simply doing what tradition tells you to do without utilizing the gifts, creativity, and energy that will emanate from investing in yourself.

What Does Investing in Yourself Mean?

You Make a Total Commitment to Yourself

It all starts with a commitment to yourself. Committing to the changes you need to make to invest in yourself can be scary, but it's best to focus on what you might gain by the change rather than what you perceive as a sacrifice.

To commit to change, you must be willing to stop making excuses. You must be willing to do things that you never have in the past, and to see them through!

Develop Confidence in Yourself

In his book, "Millionaire Success Habits," Dean Graziosi interviewed the legendary Tony Robbins. Robbins said,

"There's no way in hell you're going to have a lasting success on a large scale without confidence, because without confidence you're not going to take massive action. Massive action, learning from what doesn't work, changing your approach until you get where you want is really what makes someone succeed in the long term in any context."

It takes a lot of confidence to determine that you will go from the life you have now to the life you want, from the Misplaced life to the Motivated life. When you invest in yourself, you do the things that help you cultivate the confidence to move forward. The only way to continuously gain confidence is to grow beyond where you are today, to keep making progress, and to keep growing towards your goals.

Be Cognizant of With Whom You Spend Time

Investing in yourself includes taking a good look at those around you. Are these the type of individuals who will support a transition in your life? Will they support your mission and your goals to live a Motivated life? Will they understand that you are taking the steps necessary to create the life that you want? Will they support you? At the very least, will they get out the way and not work against your efforts?

These are all important things for you to think about because, in life, we end up becoming the sum total of the people with whom we spend the most amount of time. On your new journey, you cannot afford to surround yourself with people who are naysayers; full of drama and negativity. Sadly, some people are under the impression that if you begin to shine, it somehow diminishes their own light. They're more content being around people who they view as beneath them because they enjoy a feeling of superiority.

If people in your life are not supporting your goals with encouraging words, sound advice, positive reinforcement, and reasonable help when requested, it might be time to invite some new people into your life.

Never Stop Pursuing Self-Education

Whenever you study the successful habits of millionaires and business owners, you will realize that one of the main habits they stress is their commitment to learning and reading books. Many of them say that their reading time is a guarded priority in their life. Why? Because when they read, they learn, and they grow from what they learn. Reading is the main way they self-educate.

You simply cannot go wrong with self-education. Always keep in mind the famous quote by Jim Rohn:

> **"Formal education will make you a living; self-education will make you a fortune."**

In one form or another, directly or indirectly, you will always use the information you gain from self-education. If you are a young person, during the course of your life, you will be amazed at how many times you will recall something you read in the past, which is applicable in your life or in the life of someone you want to help. Reading books, such as this one, that provides you with guidance and necessary information to change your life, should be a constant in the foundation of your Motivated life.

Think about this simple fact—all of the things that you want to achieve in order to live your Motivated life have already been attained by others. Unless you want to be the first person on Saturn, there isn't anything that you want that hasn't already been attained by someone else. And, the methods to get on the paths taken by those individuals are, more often than not, provided in books. In their books, the men and women who have chosen to walk the path to success share their methods, which are often called "secrets to success." They share what they did, how they did it and what it felt like. How they got the help they needed, and so forth. So, the secret to your success lies within those pages, and the sooner you start learning those secrets, the better off you will be. Readers are leaders in the end.

Seek out an excellent coach in the area where you need help. A coach can save you a lifetime of frustration and help you avoid many mistakes. Sometimes you can find out more information in one or two sessions with a coach than you can after reading ten books. With a coach, you can seek and garner specific, timely information and advice that is relevant to your life or business.

You might need a life coach to help you get over specific hurdles, a financial coach to help you get your financial life in order and manage it well, or a coach that is specific to another one of your goals. The life-changing dynamic of working with a coach is well worth the time and money you will invest.

Your need for self-education might extend beyond reading on your own, mentorship, and coaching. You might need to seek out an apprenticeship or take courses to expand your skill set. As an example, if your goal is to become an entrepreneur to have the freedom to set your own schedule so that you can spend more time with your family, you might need to take some business classes (if you don't understand the business side of your service). Again, seek out community college classes and online classes. Invite professionals in the field out to lunch and find out what you need to know in order to operate the business that you want to start.

Take Charge of Your Financial Future

This was briefly mentioned earlier, but it's also raised here because taking control of your finances is an integral part of investing in you. Outside of your health, which is not a main topic of this book because there is a plethora of great health books out there, there is no other area so closely linked to the quality of your Motivated life than your financial intelligence. The world is filled with people who aren't living their dreams or purpose, largely due to their lack of financial education. Because of this tragedy, they are stuck living a life of servitude to their job and bills. Everything that they can plan for and do in their lives is based solely on serving their job just to pay their bills. This can be a tough way to live. People wonder why their life turned out this way—why all they do is work and still have very little time to do the things that matter most to them. For many people, even when they achieve the next promotion, they aren't any happier or more fulfilled. They still lack passion and satisfaction with the way that their life is unfolding. Although these people wonder how they got to this point in their lives, they unfortunately don't acknowledge that the only one holding them back is themselves.

It's critical for you to invest in yourself and take full responsibility for your financial intelligence. If you want your financial picture to change, you must pick up the paint brush and paint a different picture. If you're not willing to do that, the picture won't change for the better. Don't wait around for someone else to paint your financial picture for you. Even if you have a wonderful career and are relying on your organization to continue providing a handsome salary and comfortable retirement, be prepared because things could change without any notice, and your whole life could be dramatically different in an instant. You probably have already seen this happen to your friends, family or co-workers. It might have even happened to you.

How can you take charge of your finances? You will find information to help you with this question later in the book. For now, grasp the fact that you must take responsibility for your financial intelligence.

Invest in Your Health

If you invested in a million-dollar race horse, would you allow it to live an unhealthy lifestyle? Would you let it get insufficient sleep, eat unhealthy food, drink alcohol and smoke? Of course, you wouldn't.

But, are you treating your body with any less respect than a million-dollar race horse? If you had a million-dollar race horse, you would take care of it. You would make sure that it exercised daily, had healthy nutrition, adequate rest, and would limit anything that might detract from its optimal performance. If that's the case, why would you treat your body with any less of a commitment?

Diet and exercise are usually things that people don't like discussing. However, they both affect every function of the human body. You don't have to be an athlete or a fitness fanatic to get adequate daily exercise. Take a walk or hike; play ball with the kids; join a sports team; do something active for entertainment instead of sitting. America's favorite recreation seems to be watching movies. There's nothing wrong with watching movies, occasionally. But watching movies is not active. It doesn't benefit your body, and in fact, sitting too long for the majority of each day might even be harmful to your body. Many are now saying that sitting has become the new smoking!

The key here is to be aware that exercise can be fun, and good nutrition can be enormously beneficial. Develop that mindset so that you won't dread exercising. Try to think of ways you can turn exercise and movement of your body into fun! Exercise is necessary for a healthy, well-functioning body. Don't lie to yourself and think that you are the one and only human who can function at your very best without movement and some form of activity in your life.

Seek out information for a healthy eating plan that is composed of real food prepared in its most natural form. Find a healthy plan that fits your lifestyle, budget, schedule for cooking, *etc*. You don't have to be in the kitchen all of the time in order to eat healthy and enjoyable meals. You must get past your desires for unhealthy, sugary, fried, processed, and chemical-laden foods. Again, consistency builds good habits. Start small. Maybe start by eating a healthy breakfast instead of stopping by the doughnut shop. Work your way toward having a sit-down breakfast with your spouse or family before you leave for the office. Maybe start by cutting out high-calorie, sugar and chemical-laden soda and replacing it with water or unsweetened iced tea. If you have a habit of eating too much food, maybe begin by cutting out snacks, or cutting your meal portions in half. Start now, any way that you can, and change your eating habits. Then, take one step after another until your diet is clean and one that fuels your body for optimum life enjoyment and productivity. You cannot live the Motivated life without enjoying optimal health.

It's beyond the scope of this book to address health issues in detail. This section is included to make you aware that you must invest in your health if you want to be strong enough to be successful in reaching your goals and realizing your dreams. If you want to go for long-term success, stop and take a good look at how you're treating your mind, body, and emotions, and do whatever it takes to become healthy and remain healthy.

Find a Business Coach or a Mentor

Nobody achieves success on their own. No matter who you are, having someone else who can help direct and support you is key in all phases of life. Those people are especially important when you feel down, experience failure (which you inevitably will), or simply feel at a loss for your next step. You need an advocate who has already experienced what you're going through. Knowing that someone fully understands what you are feeling can help. Plus, they can also explain the path they took that got them to the other side of their own setbacks. It's encouraging when you can talk with someone and see that since they made it through, so can you. It helps you set aside any excuses and reasons you might have for not being able to make it. It energizes you to evaluate where you are, where you want to go, and take the next step.

Many highly successful people acknowledge and give credit to the coach or mentor who helped guide them on their path to success. These successful people maintain a sense of gratitude for the help they have received. They are not insecure people who think that having a coach or mentor is a sign of weakness. They realize the value of a coach.

It's your ego that tells you that you can do everything on your own, without anyone else's help. Egos can be troublemakers trying to lead you down the wrong path! No matter who you are or what you have accomplished in life, there is always something that you can learn from someone else. Be open-minded toward those who can offer you sound advice and who can be a sounding board for your problems. Sometimes, all you need is something as simple as a different perspective. As an example, in order to move to the next level, you might need some financial advice. Effective mentors and business coaches have bright lights to shine on the crevices where you seem to be stuck. Humble yourself and work alongside those who can help you.

Build Valuable Relationships

Professional relationships are a key element of any successful person's life. Developing professional relationships creates a sense of responsibility among team members. Working alongside other professionals with whom you have a meaningful relationship makes the work more meaningful, challenges you, and causes you to do your best work.

As a professional or entrepreneur, it's beneficial to form relationships with co-workers, entrepreneurs, partners, superiors, suppliers, customers, investors, community leaders, industry leaders, and so forth.

How do you create professional and personal relationships?

Perhaps Dale Carnegie knew "the secret" and summed it up well when he said, "You can make more friends in two months by becoming interested in other people than you can in two years by trying to get other people interested in you."

It's simple. When you show a sincere interest in people and in what they are doing, you're off to a good start with building a relationship. Take the time to notice, ask questions, and listen to what those with whom you have relationships have to say. To gain a friend, you must be a friend.

Focus on Ways to Give Back

When you give back, it acknowledges your care for humanity. It causes you to think outside of yourself and expand your boundaries. Giving back is a way of investing in your yourself. In addition to benefiting you, giving back provides others with the opportunity to grow and expand their lives. You, in turn, will reap the reward of having been a part of that growth.

How can you give back? Share what you know. Teach what you have learned in local schools, business groups, after-school clubs, and through online courses. Write books to share your knowledge. Be an influencer and help change lives through sharing what you know.

For entrepreneurs who are just launching their business, mentoring high school or college students can add tremendous value to their lives. In a professional manner, spend time with the one(s) you mentor. Become genuinely interested in their goals and take the time to meet with them as needed.

In conclusion, investing in yourself is up to you. Nobody will do it for you. The steps you take to invest in you helps you position yourself for success on your Motivated journey.

Motivated Thinking from Chapter 9:	<ul><li>Investing in yourself is the single best investment.</li><li>Self-education will make you rich.</li><li>Focusing on your physical health pays dividends.</li></ul>

- A business or personal coach can be extremely beneficial in helping you transition from a Misplaced life to a Motivated life.
- Invest in relationships and surround yourself with those who help support your dream.
- Always give back as a way of investing in yourself.

Chapter 10:

Step 3

Create the Right Goals for You

"If you want to be happy, set a goal that commands your thoughts, liberates your energy, and inspires your hopes."

~Andrew Carnegie

In his very informative article in Psychology Today magazine, science writer and public education specialist David DiSalvo notes that your brain is a goal-setting machine. It's actually designed for goal-setting and achievement. Over the years, scores of studies have shown over the years, the value in having goals. However, you have to do more than just have a mental list. In order for your goal setting to be successful, you must realize that:

- Setting specific goals and writing them down is critical.
- Repeating a goal makes it stick.
- Achieving your goals boosts your self-confidence.
- It takes time to work achieve most goals.
- Set backs are not failures.

There are many books on goal-setting but most of them yield the exact opposite results of what they're setting out to accomplish. So, let's try something different for you. Let's not have you sit and create a three- or five-year plan. That will come one day, but it's not the ideal place to begin. Creating that type of plan can sap your creative energy before you even get started. Goals shouldn't be about checklists; they should be about dreaming. They should inspire you to be the person that you know you can be, not a constant reminder that you aren't living up to your potential. Goals are merely a description of a journey that you would like to take. And, when you think of them, you should be excited to be on that journey.

So, let's make this fun for you, but also productive and life-changing.

When the best and brightest minds sit in a boardroom and talk about building a great company, they do what Stephen Covey encouraged years ago; they begin with the end in mind. They ask themselves these kind of questions:

- How do we build the world's best company in our market?
- If we lead the market in the future, what kind of company will we have built?
- What would it look like?
- How would it operate?
- How would it outsmart its competition?
- How would it be the best at serving its customers?
- What types of products would it market?
- What types of people would it need?
- How would it constantly innovate?
- How could it differentiate itself from others?
- How can it protect its lead?

And on and on.

This process is used first to envision the particular attributes that define a great company. Then, the great minds begin working backwards on their plan in order to achieve what was envisioned. Eventually, both a short and long-term plan will evolve. However, prior to any plans is the vision, a dream, something to get excited about. If you don't have that, you won't be able to make progress, and without measurable progress, the effort will eventually stop.

You have to think about yourself in a similar way. Before you think about the timing milestones, dates, and steps to achieve your goals, you need a vision of yourself to use as a guide.

Your Vision

You know what's great about you? That you are you! You are a unique individual. Your vision is not exactly the same as anyone else's vision. Your vision is yours. What you see as the Motivated version of you is what's relevant in all areas of your life. So first, let's focus on that, and then work backwards on how to get there. The most important thing that anyone can do to help you with your goals is to assist you with your vision and get you launched. The rest comes as it comes.

The Steps

While you are going through your steps, it's important for you to write down your thoughts. Buy a hard-bound journal or use some type of notebook that is a gift to yourself. Your notebook can be any type of notebook, but make sure that it's a dedicated notebook that won't be used for anything else. Nobody else should have access to it; this is about you! Opening your notebook should be a signal that helps you drown out the normal daily fluctuations and distractions of life. Think of your notebook as a place that you go to rather than just a notebook. For you, perhaps, it's a little secluded spot in the mountains where you can think and watch the forest animals. Maybe your spot is an abandoned beach where you sit and listen to the ocean waves roll in, drowning out all of your thoughts and stresses of normal daily life. Just imagine your spot and go there when you take out your notebook to write. It's your place where no person one or anything else enters. You are the keeper of the gate, and each time you enter the spot, you put up the 'do not disturb' sign to prevent distractions from cluttering your mind.

Have your notebook and pen easily accessible without having to search for it each time. Do not use a PC or mobile device for this exercise. You can codify all of this at a later time in a number of places, but for now it's just you, your pen, and paper. Handwriting on paper was sufficient for founding a country, so it's certainly a good enough method for building a new you. Besides that, there is a significant amount of scientific evidence indicating that writing longhand on paper can be beneficial by helping you: feel less distracted, learn faster, exercise more creativity, and keep your mind in better mental condition. So, put away your laptop or tablet, and get out your special notebook, pens and markers.

A) Envision the Motivated You

Find a quiet place where others won't interrupt you and where you won't become distracted by noises and conversations. Label the first five pages of your journal with the following five areas of life, because the first thing you will record in your journal will be recorded in one of these five categories:

- Presence
- Physical
- Financial

- Spiritual
- Life Adventures

Close your eyes and see yourself as the person that only you know you can be. This vison was instilled in you a long time ago. Perhaps you tucked it away for one reason or another and you haven't nurtured the vision of this person. Your vision of the person might seem vague and blurry to you at first, or it might even feel distant, as though you're seeing someone else in your mind. If it's been a long time since you thought about that person, you might ask yourself, who is that person? That person might seem very different from the person you are today.

Don't think about anything else. It probably will take a few minutes or longer to stop all of the thoughts that bombard your mind and interrupt that vision. When you are at your quiet place, that is not the time to think about your list of errands, like how you will change your schedule to accommodate the extra work you need to do tomorrow; who will pick up the kids from school; or where you'll go on vacation. It's not the time to create a to-do list in your mind. If you're like most people, you probably have a million things on your mind at all times, and you will try to multi-task while you're writing in your journal. However, in order to achieve the best results, resist those temptations. Your mind will probably fight you when you try to turn off the thoughts. Keep resisting those intrusions. Keep focusing on that person whom you are visualizing and let that person come into focus in your mind. This might not fully happen the first time you sit to write. If it doesn't, don't fret about it. It will become easier with each successive attempt at focusing.

As you focus on the person that you want to become, continue envisioning yourself in various scenarios when you actually have the result you always wanted. Work on focusing your mind and envisioning yourself in various scenarios such as having your dream job; being the parent you want to be; traveling to the countries you always wanted to visit; inventing the things you want to invent; helping others; speaking before large audiences; receiving an award for your humanitarian work; being healthy; succeeding in your business; overcoming a personal obstacle, *etc.*

As you see yourself in that positive light, ask yourself the following questions, and write down your thoughts as they appear to you.

Key Questions to Ask:

- How do you see yourself as the successful version of you?
- How many solid relationships do you have?
- What do you look like?
- How do you act?
- What pursuits do you enjoy?
- What have you conquered for you?
- What career do you have?
- How do you speak?
- What your body look like?
- How do you dress and present yourself?
- What is your financial position?
- What is your spiritual position?
- How do you treat others?
- What type of examples do you set for others?
- How do you inspire others?

Try to see yourself in front of a room filled with young people giving a talk on success; what are you saying to them? Think about each question and let the details come to your mind.

As you write down your thoughts, remember to put them into the five simple categories with which you labeled the first pages of your journal: Presence, Physical, Financial, Spiritual, and Life Adventures.

Presence

You start with presence because it shows you the end goal, and then you can work backwards. You need to envision a successful and Motivated version of yourself from every aspect of life. The person that you see is successful and living a Motivated life. That successful person is positive, inspirational, takes care of their body, has a financial plan, cultivates and maintains excellent relationships, and lives a spiritual life based on giving back to others and sharing what they have learned.

You need to capture and encapsulate as many details as possible. How you look, feel, the shape that you're in, the financial intelligence that you have, and how you live as an inspiring example to others. Write down as many specifics as you can and be as descriptive as possible. Try to fill at least one page with your thoughts.

Physical

How does the Motivated version of you look and feel physically? Instead of a face that is tense with stress, are you smiling and is there a sparkle in your eye? Do you look well-rested and energetic? Have you traded in your drab black office wear for handsome/pretty colorful attire that better suits your cheerful personality?

What type of nutrition and fitness plan do you follow? Instead of flopping on the sofa exhausted after work, eating a greasy, fast-food dinner, are you putting on your sneakers and walking two miles before you sit down to a dinner of healthy vegetables and lean meat? Instead of passively watching sports on TV on the weekend, are you meeting friends to play a game of basketball out in the sunshine at the park? Instead of consuming doughnuts and coffee drinks for breakfast, are you taking the time to eat a high-protein breakfast that fuels you with sufficient energy throughout your morning? What type of activity do you fit in daily to make certain that your physical body is part of your successful life? Be as descriptive as you can. Try to fill at least one page with your thoughts.

Financial

How is the Motivated version of you positioned financially? Have you created multiple streams of income, so that you feel secure about paying all of your bills each month? Are you saving money, knowing that you will be able to take care of your family if your main job suddenly disappears? Is everything lining up for you to purchase a new home that is large enough for your growing family? Are you retired, living a life of freedom and comfort? Are you financially secure and free from a limiting work schedule, with an adequate budget to travel without worry?

What type of financial plan do you follow? Are you investing? Are you sticking to your budget and insisting that your family stick to it too? Do you invest money in various ways so that you aren't dependent on one investment type? What type of financial success have you achieved? What are your financial goals and aspirations? How do you use your financial achievement to benefit yourself?

Spiritual

How is the Motivated version of you serving as an example to others? Do you meditate? Do you go to a house of worship? Do you pray? Do your core beliefs and the way you live your life line up? How are you giving back? Are you donating money, time, or knowledge to people, causes, and organizations that are meaningful to you? Are you practicing gratitude? Are you living a life of integrity?

Life Adventures

Life is about passion, fun, and experiencing new things. How is the Motivated version of you living your life? Are you managing your time well and guarding your time for relaxation and fun? Do you see yourself closing the laptop at a reasonable hour in the evening and focusing on having fun with your family or friends, working on a hobby, attending a group function that you enjoy, or watching a funny movie? What fun and exciting things are you doing? What places do you plan to visit? What sports do you play? Are you doing any activities? Do you have hobbies? Are you doing something that you were afraid to do before? Are you stretching your horizons to include new activities?

Writing down thoughts is not everyone's forte. Just know that the more you write, the easier it will become. Soon, there will come a time when you will eagerly take out your notebook to write.

B) Designing the Steps to Achieve Your Motivated Life

In each of the areas above, read your notes over several times and as you are reading, write down the response to this question: What are the top three things that I will need to do in order to achieve that which the Motivated person I have envisioned has already achieved?

List the three top things for each of the following areas: 1) Presence, 2) Physical, 3) Financial, 4) Spiritual, and 5) Life Adventures. Only list three things. These should be the top three things in each area that would move you closer to the Motivated person that you have envisioned. It greatly helps to make the three things as specific, concise, and clear as possible. They need to be things that you can use to create tactics for your life. For example, in the financial area, it could be that the Motivated version of you is financially intelligent and understands the key principles of investing for your future.

C) Creating Your Plan of Action

You now have fifteen goals that you need to focus in order to achieve the level of success that you saw in the Motivated version of yourself. These fifteen items are the foundation of your Motivated life plan and as of today, these are your personal and individualized goals. See how easy it was to set those goals? If you find a way to achieve them, you will be the person that you envisioned. These are your unique areas of focus. Now, let's go one step further to help your mind with attainment.

For each of these fifteen goals, list one thing that you can do daily, monthly, and yearly to achieve the desired outcome. Be specific, but also make sure that what you list can fit into your life. For example, if you already work 60 hours a week, listing that you will read one financial education book every week might be setting yourself up for disappointment. Or, if you are recovering from a medical condition that limits mobility, listing that you will walk one mile every day is not realistic for you at this time.

For your plan to work, you need to experience your progress, so be realistic with what you can accomplish daily, monthly, and yearly. You can always alter the plan later if you're over-achieving, but for now, give yourself the ability to get some immediate wins. Wins will help you build good habits, gain momentum, and move forward. It will also help train your mind to stay focused on your plan.

D) Execution

Execution of your plan is the part where most people fail. It's one thing to write down a plan in a journal, and another thing to execute the plan. You can be excited about the plan and really want the plan to happen, but if you don't execute the plan, nothing will happen. You won't be any closer to becoming the Motivated person that you desire. And yet, it doesn't have to be complicated. Simply list the goals and tactics that you've designed into the following areas:

- **Daily Goals**
- **Monthly Goals**

- **Yearly Goals**

Write them in such a way as to ensure that you can easily follow your progress. You might want to get creative and put them into a bullet-style journal or you may want to use a simple spreadsheet style. Do whatever works best for you to have the visual that you need in order to track your progress toward achieving your goals.

Congratulations, if you've made it this far, you've already done more on goal setting and designing your Motivated life than nine out of ten people in the world! You should be proud of yourself and know that you can do this. You're off to a great start!

Motivated Thinking from Chapter 10:

- Goals are pivotal to your future success.
- In order for goals to work for you, they need to be specific and in written form.
- Your goals should be about your dream for yourself and your future.
- You can easily set goals by envisioning yourself as the Motivated person you want to become.
- Set your goals for the following important areas: 1) Presence, 2) Physical, 3) Financial, 4) Spiritual, and 5) Life Adventures.

Chapter 11:

Step 4

Think Like an Entrepreneur

"To change your life, you have to change yourself. To change yourself, you have to change your mindset."

~Anonymous

In her article in Forbes titled "We Are All Entrepreneurs: It's A Mindset, Not A Business Model," Donna M. De Carolis, Ph.D., the founding dean of the Charles D. Close School of Entrepreneurship at **Drexel University** notes that "Being entrepreneurial is essentially about thinking and doing something that we have not done before, in order to achieve a desirable goal or outcome. It is about assessing a situation, designing alternatives, and choosing a new way -- or perhaps a combination of ways -- that we hope will lead us to something better."

The advice in this book is not only for the entrepreneur, but for anyone that wants to further his or her success by thinking more like that of the entrepreneur. In fact, the qualities and traits of a successful entrepreneur are the same qualities that are necessary to live a "Motivated" life full of inspiration and passion, no matter what your life's dream is to become. The same qualities possessed by successful entrepreneurs can serve you well in whatever arena you function, whether it's a corporate job, service job, non-profit volunteer, *etc.*

Why is this so? Because an entrepreneur believes that he or she is in control. In fact, entrepreneurs are not comfortable when someone else is in control of their life, finances, time, etc. While they are disciplined enough to move forward and take care of their responsibilities, entrepreneurs have a difficult time staying within the limitations that others set for them because they believe that the sky is the limit with what they can accomplish. They believe in themselves! No matter what you pursue in your Motivated life, you'll need to believe in yourself and know that you can be successful. You will need to understand that you can succeed because you choose to do so, and that you are willing to put in the work and time required to be successful. You fully comprehend that you don't need anyone's permission to live your Motivated life and be successful.

Entrepreneurs are creative dreamers who are determined to make their dreams come true. They are able to calculate risk and move forward with the self-education of how to minimize that risk in order to execute their plan. They feel that the sky is the limit because they believe in themselves and in the vision they have for themselves. Entrepreneurs rely on themselves and on a circle of trustworthy and supportive people who won't let them down.

Entrepreneurs are confident that they can and will create the circumstances that they want in life. Rather than allowing circumstances to define who they are, they take the reins and determine their circumstances. They don't wait for anything to be given to them. They go out and create what they want.

If they ever need help in fulfilling their vision, Motivated people and entrepreneurs get the help they need. However, they will always remain the captain of their own ship to ensure that they are not subjected to the whims and downfalls of others. They understand that teamwork is important, and they can work well with others.

Some aspects of the entrepreneurial mindset actually make many people uncomfortable because they are contrary to what they have been taught. The entrepreneur is comfortable with unconventional thinking. They thrive when they are challenged to think outside the box and discover new possibilities. Possibilities may be an entrepreneur's favorite word, and they look for opportunity and possibilities at all times.

Entrepreneurs are leaders rather than followers. They are independent enough to do whatever work needs to be done in order to accomplish their goals. This is true even when the work is different from what they usually do. They realize the benefit of gaining the perspectives of other people and actively seek out what others have learned. They know they don't have to reinvent the wheel, but they are not afraid to be creative and put forth their best ideas, even when those ideas might be met with ridicule, at first.

Earlier in this book, we made the point that the classic educational system can easily leave you with a certain set of passive traits that should be replaced with a different set of traits later in life. The sooner the better—that is, if you want to live a Motivated life where you are in charge of your time, finances, and how you live every day. The initial blueprint for this process is what this chapter is all about. The following five areas, if they become traits in your life, will significantly change the outcomes that you achieve.

The Entrepreneurial Mindset Begins with Constantly Evolving Education

Entrepreneurs invest in self-education. They realize a very simple truth in life. They acknowledge that in almost every conceivable case, what they are trying to accomplish has already been accomplished by someone else. Therefore, the logical and efficient process is to learn from those individuals and copy their steps. It doesn't have to be any more complicated than that.

If you want to be successful, you have to make the time and have the discipline to learn from others, formally or informally. Learning is an ongoing process that never stops in life. You will never learn everything that there is to learn. The moment that you think you are finished learning is the moment you are making a costly mistake. You must continue to learn, no matter how many degrees you have or how old you are. If you are currently on the wrong path, view it as an indication that you need to learn some new strategies, meet some new people, and then correct your present course.

Don't beat yourself up if you're on the wrong path. Scolding and punishing yourself won't help you get on the right path. Hanging your head low, walking in embarrassment, and apologizing for what others deem as failures won't position you to succeed in your endeavors. Take this opportunity to view the wrong path you are on as an invitation to get on the right path. Learning some new strategies or skills may seem like an obvious next step. However, many people are oblivious to this next step. It's easier to cling to what you know in the hopes that it will somehow magically yield a better result one day. It doesn't work that way. Hoping that it does work that way is the mindset that keeps people on the Misplaced path.

It's easy to recognize when others aren't learning new strategies and are continuing to fail by remaining on their same Misplaced path. It's much more difficult to recognize or admit that you aren't learning the new strategies you need. Think about people you know who have had the same problems or frustrations for many years. Perhaps they call you every week with the same issues, asking you to help them find a solution. Perhaps they corner you at work and reiterate the problem to make sure you understand that they are still having the same problems. It might be easy for YOU to realize that they need a self-development class to learn how to overcome their issue. They don't or won't see that they need help so they simply continue doing the same thing by living the same way. By not reacting and making changes, they, themselves, are ensuring that the problem will persist.

Meanwhile, you, yourself might be on a path where someone else is controlling important areas of your life. You, too, might feel frustrated about it, but you continue to remain on the path anyway. Why? Probably because you didn't learn new strategies to help you get off the wrong path and onto the right one. You have to be willing to learn new strategies. You must seek out the information you need that will help you make changes in your life.

We can learn something about how self-development can help solve problems in one's Motivated life when we take a look at a problem that Thomas had, and see how he solved that problem using new self-development information. Thomas was a mid-level manager at a national corporation. He liked his job and worked hard at it. Sadly, when Thomas was only three years away from retirement, the company went through a restructuring process and Thomas' department was outsourced. His job was eliminated. Without a job or any solid prospects, Thomas took the opportunity (and risk) to use his retirement fund to start the business he always dreamed of having.

After several sessions with a business coach, Thomas did the prerequisite work to launch his business. Everything in his business went well, except for one thing: The employee turnover was very high, and employee acquisition and training was costing the company a fortune. On average, new hires remained with the company for less than six months, and many new hires left within three months of joining the team. Thomas could not figure out why he could not retain employees. He paid a competitive salary, offered a nice benefits package, and thought he was doing a good job as a business owner and general manager of the company.

Thomas knew he could not afford to continue investing in training new employees so frequently, so he met with his business coach to discuss the problem. The business coach agreed to pop in as an observer at Thomas' business a few times to see whether he could determine the root of the problem. The coach also helped Thomas write a questionnaire about the workplace, for the employees to answer anonymously.

After visiting the business only one time, the business coach told Thomas that the problem with employee retention was obvious. When the questionnaires were returned, it became evident to Thomas that he was the reason he could not retain employees. Thomas learned that he was a very poor communicator, and that his poor communication skills resulted in the employees not doing their tasks properly. When the job was not done properly, Thomas exploded, blamed the employees and threatened to fire them.

The employees suffered from Thomas' poor communication and management style. They felt humiliated in front of their co-workers. Workplace morale was low. Everyone ducked their heads and just tried to get through their work day without being admonished. The employees lacked job security because they never knew when they might be doing something wrong and find their own heads on the chopping block. Since many of them feared losing their job at any moment, they found other jobs and quit before they could be terminated.

Thomas was mortified that he had done such a poor job of managing his staff, particularly since his former career had been in management. His previous management career had been with a company that used old-school management methods that included browbeating, yelling, and threatening employees. That is what Thomas was accustomed to doing, and at his old company, he had the backing of his superiors for his poor behavior. They had always blamed the employees and considered them to be fickle and disloyal when they left the company, never stopping to think and realize why they actually left.

When Thomas acknowledged that he had to adopt a different management style and gain new strategies for communicating with his employees, Thomas swallowed his pride and faced his staff. He apologized to his employees, explaining that he didn't realize that he was behaving in the negative manner uncovered by his business coach and on the questionnaire. He made a commitment to his staff that, if they would remain with the company, he would seek out self-development and management training to change his management style, improve his communication skills, learn to control his temper, and learn how to treat the staff with respect. He offered a bonus to those who had the courage to walk the self-improvement path with him for the next three months.

Change can be scary and uncomfortable. Most do not self-educate or create new strategies to change what they need to change in order to achieve better results. Most people prefer to believe that they are comfortable enough with their known world and unhappy ways, rather than make some uncomfortable changes to achieve their happier and more fulfilled Motivated life. The unknown can seem worse than the discomfort of living a life you don't love, or even like. The thing to remember is that the unknown is only the unknown until you take the necessary steps to turn the unknown into the known. That's a mouthful to say, but it's a simple concept to grasp. Once you take a step toward getting out of your comfort zone, you'll build momentum to continue learning new strategies and moving forward with changing your life.

Some people are not motivated enough to take the steps to achieve a Motivated life. Those people usually approach life with an attitude of if it's not broken don't fix it. They usually take what they assume will be the easiest path, with the least resistance. Sadly, these types of people either live in denial that their life is broken, or they don't realize just how broken it is. They have refused to let themselves dream of a better life. They have either forgotten or have never learned what it feels like to have enthusiasm and passion for their life. They are resigned to being okay without the freedom to choose what they want for themselves in life, letting whatever happens to them, happen to them.   They've given up on finding the strategies to be in control of the life they want to live.

Some people are too lazy to make any changes, so they choose to live their predictable lives, even though they might be miserable. They may not realize, or even care, that the lazy life doesn't usually lead to a fulfilling life or that it might be requiring them to pay a very high price in many ways. Even though there are plenty of examples all around them, they don't acknowledge that lazy people are often miserable, Misplaced people. Even though there are many strategies to deal with laziness, those who are lazy settle for remaining as they are rather than self-educating on how to overcome laziness and change their lives for the better.

Entrepreneurs know that a happy life, well-lived, takes energy and perseverance. It doesn't happen automatically, and it's not always easy. It isn't handed to anyone, but it is available to everyone who is willing to self-educate and incorporate the strategies for a happy life. Below, you'll find eight key mantras of successful Motivated people and entrepreneurs.

Eight Key Characteristics of the Entrepreneur

1. Think Like an Owner and Take Responsibility

This applies to all areas of your life, health, wealth, and happiness. Life doesn't have to just happen to you as though you have no say so about what you do or where you end up. As a human being with free-will, you have the power and ability to decide what you do and how you live. Don't be passive in life; choose to be active. Be active in determining what you want and how you will use your skills to achieve those things. When a novice writer attends writing classes or becomes involved in a writing group, one of the first things they are taught is to show, don't tell. This means, instead of passively telling a story, put the character in the story and show the character living the story. Instead of passively telling the story of what you are going to accomplish someday, start living your story TODAY! Today, start owning your story and be a willing and eager participant in the story.

Nobody says you have to stay on the path you are on if it's not the right one for you. As Jim Rohn says, "If you don't like how things are, change it. You are not a tree." You are never planted too deeply to dig up your roots and replant yourself on a better path.

You must realize that you are the boss of you and you can decide to make changes at any time. That's one of the great liberties of becoming an independent adult. You can always change the path—without the world coming to an end. What will others think? It doesn't matter. Other people are not responsible for your life, you are.

You don't have to stay in your current job/career, toxic relationships, negative environment, unhealthy lifestyle, poor financial situation, *etc*. Don't sit back and just accept the way things are if you aren't happy or feel that your life is not headed in the direction you want. Educate yourself on how to change your path to become your happy, "Motivated Self." Please note that I am not advocating that you act irresponsibly if you have a family to take care of, or if you have other obligations that prevent you from making big changes all at once. In those scenarios, you must take logical steps to ensure that everybody continues to be cared for during your transition to becoming your Motivated self. But today, you can responsibly take a big step toward living your Motivated life by simply deciding that you are going to change your life and that you will be investing in yourself to self-educate. This will give you the ability to make the necessary changes as soon as you can do so responsibly, without negatively impacting your dependents.

The Entrepreneurial Mindset is based on the idea that you are the CEO of you! So, when you get involved in anything, you need to view the initiatives as though you were the owner. To insert a popular phrase—you have to own it like a boss! How would you "own it" if you were the CEO of a national, multi-million-dollar corporation? Would you slink around in the background, hoping that everything worked out? Would you be lazy and neglect your duties? Would you tiptoe around thinking that perhaps one day you might take the next step to bring the company to the next level? No! The smart leader, and the one who wants to meet their goals, doesn't wait around for things to work out. They own their stage. They come out front and take control and responsibility. They utilize every skill and tool in their possession to make certain that things will work out for the best for themselves, their company, and their staff.

When considering your position at work, you need to think about what the boss thinks about. Don't only think of the tasks you perform. Train your mind to think about all of the bigger issues facing your company on a daily basis. Start thinking about how successful your company is in the marketplace; what the next steps should be; how you can influence others to meet their goals; and so forth. You should think about how strong your business is versus its competition and the vibrancy of its core business model. Once you start thinking at this high level, it will be challenging to turn your mind back to a daily operating role, and that's the point! Entrepreneurs look at every endeavor as if they own it, and that they are in control of it. They accept personal responsibility for its success or failure.

You can easily apply this way of thinking to all the areas of your life, whether it's wealth, health, or even relationships. When you think about it, you have to agree that your result in each of these areas is directly proportional to the extent you owned that area by accepting responsibility and learning how to achieve a great outcome by doing the necessary work.

2. Take Risks and Don't Fear Failure

If you are like most people, you were taught that failure is a bad thing. It illustrates how you, or another person with whom you were involved, put forward an effort that didn't work out the way you wanted it to work out, and you now have a bad result or nothing at all to show for it. Failures are often viewed as wasted time, energy, and resources, but nothing could be further from the truth. Failure is not a bad thing!

Failure is an attempt at something (action) and a learning experience (knowledge) that teaches you that you need to take a different course of action in order to achieve success. In this mode of thinking, what is often labeled as failure can be a gift. Think of scientists and inventors and the many failures they have experienced before achieving the positive results they seek. They conduct many experiments before they get it right. Where would they be if they viewed every unsuccessful experiment or invention as a failure? Would they be able to continue in their work if they failed so often that they started to think of themselves as a failure rather than a scientist or inventor? Probably not. But scientists and inventors who are determined to do their best work and reach the best possible outcome keep on experimenting. They keep looking for the solution. They don't focus on the problem. They don't give up. They know the solution is out there waiting for them to discover it. They look at what they did wrong and come up with a different and better way to achieve what they wanted.

When you get a different outcome than what you expected, don't label yourself as a failure. If you are trying, you are not a failure. Don't see yourself as a failure based on the outcomes of your experiments. Remember, you must visualize yourself as the person you want to become. If you start to visualize yourself as a failure, and you start to believe you are a failure, you will start to act like a failure instead of as a Motivated entrepreneur.

Failure represents the crossroad of knowledge and action. You can't fail without taking action and trying, and it's impossible for you to take any action and not learn something. You might not always learn what you thought you would learn, but you will always learn something when you take action. Therefore, failure truly is a learning experience, and one that should be admired and emulated, not feared.

Many highly successful people seem to become overnight successes in their field of expertise. The reality is that most successful people will tell you that it took them many years of experimenting and having what most people would call failures before they reached success. Never be ashamed of so-called failures. Think of them as part of your self-education. Reclaim your agenda and move forward!

3. Focus on Solutions, Not Problems

How easy it is to point out problems! Some people do it like there's a reward for doing it, or like they should be recognized for spotting problems rather than coming up with solutions. It's almost like some people have negative blinders on that make them see only problems and become completely blind to the fact that there are also solutions out there. The Motivated entrepreneur knows that for every problem, there is a solution.

In school, you may have been taught to study the problem. Therefore, you are likely accustomed to viewing the problem from every possible angle, trying to find the "catch" or the trick you can use to solve the problem. You soon become well acquainted with the problem. You can recite the problem by rote. Unfortunately, there seems to be no solution in sight because you have been dwelling on the problem. Your brain has been trained to puzzle the problem rather than think about solutions. Is your goal to know the problem well, or to find a solution? If your goal is to find a solution, shouldn't you train your brain to think about solutions rather than problems?

Seeing only the problems makes you common, and who wants to be like everybody else? Motivated people don't. Successful entrepreneurs don't. They're smarter than that. And, so are you! Why would anyone want to wallow around in a problem, using valuable time and energy when they can use the same valuable time and energy finding a solution?

You might not have all the answers or instantly see a solution. You should realize that when you can't figure out a solution, you can always get help. Many entrepreneurs find that hiring a business coach is a direct path to getting the help they need when they need it. Besides coaches, there are mentors, people knowledgeable in the field, co-workers, business groups, and networks that can help with finding a solution. Seeing a problem is easy. Coming up with a solution isn't always easy. That's why most people are not CEOs. That's why most people are not in charge of their lives or living a Motivated life. Ask for help when you need it. You're a Motivated human, but you are a human and we all need help at different points in our lives.

Do you think people feel better about themselves when they complain about a problem, or when they know that they worked to ultimately fix that problem? When you solve problems, you can feel proud because you have accomplished something. When you focus on the problem, there is no achievement. Focusing on problems can weigh you down, use resources, drain energy, and make time disappear that would be better used for other things. Thinking negatively can paralyze your thought process and diminish the momentum you've built for moving forward.

In all areas of your life, it's okay for you to point out the problems. After all, you need to be aware of what needs to be fixed. You need to be informed. But once you identify a problem, you need to use the skills that you presently possess or will acquire, in order to find solutions. Don't camp out at the problem campsite. Move over to the solution campsite. That's what a CEO does, and you are the CEO of you. A CEO must recognize and fix each of the problems in his or her company to ensure that it runs smoothly and yields a high profit. Isn't that what you want for yourself too?

4. Master Leadership and Influencing

The ability to lead and influence others is one of the best areas to master if you want to ensure that you'll always reach success in any area of your life. Influencing others can also be one of the most rewarding areas of living the Motivated life.

When you develop leadership skills and learn how to positively influence others, you gain the attention and time of others. This, in turn, positions you to be able to share what you know that can help lift others to a higher standard. The mark of a true leader is that they elevate the lives of those around them. All the great leaders in history have motivated others. Think about Gandhi, as an example. By directly opposing British rule, Gandhi became the symbol for freedom for his people and future generations. He has inspired and motivated generations of freedom-seeking people all over the world. Gandhi had a vision to see people free from oppression. When you have a vision, and are passionate about it, nothing can stop you from carrying out your vision. As a Motivated leader, you can influence more people than you ever dreamed of influencing.

Entrepreneurs and leaders must acknowledge the positive influence they can exercise for improving people's lives. Robert Craven, CEO of MegaFood, said in an article on New Hope Network, "My leadership philosophy all boils down to my core belief that I am personally on this planet to do something big and change the world." He went on to say, "I want to be a change-the-world CEO that works for a change-the-world company and does amazing things with change-the-world people."

Motivated entrepreneurs set out to create change. What will you stand for and do to lead and influence and make a difference in the world?

5. Build Wealth in Every Way

The Motivated entrepreneur is not narrow-minded and is not ignorant of the fact that gaining financial wealth won't automatically create the life they want. It has been said that if one is not happy before they gain wealth, they won't be happy by simply adding wealth to their life. Leaders understand that there is much more to the Motivated life than simply obtaining financial gain. They know that they must set a good foundation for their Motivated life. A happy, enriched life includes financial wealth, as well as nontangible things like the following:

- Living an authentic life.
- Living a life with the freedom to make your own choices.
- Receiving and giving of love, self, and gifts.
- Practicing gratitude.
- Having peace of mind.
- Building and maintaining healthy relationships.
- Participating in meaningful experiences.
- Expanding your thinking and experiences.
- Having a sense of purpose.
- Having a sense of self-worth.
- Being hopeful and having expectation, of good things to come.
- Fostering creativity.
- Remaining curious and continuing to learn and seek answers.
- Being content with what you have, but having the courage to improve your life.

While you are focusing on tangible steps to take to make your life a Motivated life don't forget to make time for enjoying the riches in life that have little to do with finances. You should understand that having your finances in order through entrepreneurship, can help provide you with the freedom to live a more enriched life, and with the ability to take advantage of opportunities to which you might otherwise not have had access. Having your finances in order can provide you with the freedom to influence others without any strings attached.

6. Don't Fear Change

As previously discussed, change can be scary, but self-development cannot happen without change. Either you'll change some things in your life and grow, or you'll be afraid of change and remain on your Misplaced path, and everything will remain the same. It's like the little boy who held a handful of balloons in one hand and a handful of lollipops in his other hand, when he was offered a prized toy that he had really wanted for a long time. He didn't have the courage to let go of the lollipops or the balloon strings, so he couldn't take the toy. Nothing changed for the little guy. He gave up the better prize in order to hold on to the lesser prize. How many times have you done that in your life, only to regret it later?

Change can be very good and produce results well into your future. This book can help you begin to transform your life, but only if you let them. An entrepreneurial mindset embraces change. The successful entrepreneur is not intent on everything staying the same. They are not afraid to make the changes they know are necessary.

People with the Motivated mindset welcome change, even if they must let go of something that they perceive as valuable in order to accomplish the change they want to happen in their life. Quite often, the major thing that an entrepreneur must relinquish in order to pursue the life they want is their current job. They reach a point where they either have to let go of their present position or let go of their dream. It's not a comfortable spot to be in, and no one can make that kind of decision for you. Nevertheless, you must be willing to make the change that is necessary.

Embracing change often requires sacrifice. Entrepreneurs, like you, are often faced with a choice of embracing long-term change or enjoying short-term pleasures. As an example, you might be a serious football fan and have season tickets for your favorite team. Each year, you wholeheartedly look forward to football season and going to all of the home and away games with your friends, who are also huge fans. You've been doing this for several years and it's become a tradition for you. In order to transition to a better path, you might have to skip the away games so that you can invest your weekend time in the steps to make your goals a reality. Are you willing to embrace this change, even though it means temporarily sacrificing something that you enjoy so much? Maybe your sacrifice will have to be a much more serious than missing football games. What if your new path requires that you move your family to another state? If you want to realize lasting success, you must be willing to embrace change to make it happen. Your mindset will become one where you will do everything you can, in a non-destructive and responsible manner, to make your Motivated life happen.

7. Never Trade Your Time for Money

"If you don't find a way to make money while you sleep, you will work until you die."
~Warren Buffet

That statement is very hard for some people to understand. How can you make money while you sleep? And, why should you? Moreover, isn't the only way to make money getting a job and earning a paycheck?

The concept that Buffet spoke of is two-pronged. First, in order to truly create lasting wealth, you have to focus on your net worth, not your income. Your net worth provides an accurate big picture of where you stand financially. To figure out your net worth, you simply add up all of your assets such as your home; the money in your checking and savings accounts; the value of your investment accounts; cash value of insurance policies; value of your vehicles; value of recreational vehicles; your personal valuables such as jewelry or valuable collections; business interests; and so forth. Some of you might have only one or even none of these assets and that's ok! Then, list all of your liabilities (the things you for which you owe money), such as mortgage; credit card balances; student loans; car loans; personal loans; etc. Once you have listed and calculated your total liabilities, subtract this amount from your total assets. This is your personal net worth.

Secondly, you must have multiple ways to grow your net worth, whether you're actively working or not. You have to find ways to create income whether you're in the office, lying on the beach at a tropical resort for a month, or have unexpectedly become unable to work for a season, or for the remainder of your life. Creating various streams of income is crucial for securing your financial future. Thinking that "it could never happen to me" can actually happen to anyone, including you. You need to be prepared because you never know what your future may bring. The best thing you can do is plan and prepare for a secure financial future.

When you trade your time for money, you are limiting yourself to earning money only during the time that you are actually working. Since you are a human being, and not a robot, you are limited to the number of hours you can actually work per week or month. At a job, you might be required to work a minimum of 40 to 50 hours per week for a set salary. Your hours are set and controlled by the company where you work. Your income is set and controlled by the company where you work. Without other streams of income, the company controls how much money you can make, and there is nothing beyond that. Over a life-time career, if you earn a good salary, live within your means, and save diligently, you might end up with a decent retirement—unless the company you work for determines that you are no longer a necessary part of their team, and you have to start your career over again.

Of course, entrepreneurs must work extra hours in exchange for the end result of obtaining more money and security. The difference is that entrepreneurs work to build wealth rather than simply to acquire a specified paycheck. As an example, if you work for national Company ABC, and your salary is $80,000 per year and, you are limited to earning $80,000 for the year, nothing more. As an entrepreneur, the sky is the limit for your potential annual income. Your business might see a profit of $80,000 in the first three to six months!

At your $80,000 per year job, if you're an excellent money manager and disciplined saver, and you are able to save the recommended 20% ($16,000) of your income per year, you are limited to saving only that amount. You also might be sacrificing a lot of "living" just to save that amount each year. Most people don't save 20% of their annual income or even close to that. According to a CNBC article, most Americans save only 5% or less of their income (NerdWallet 2017). While this is certainly better than saving nothing, nobody can build true, lasting wealth by saving 5% of their limited income per year. Remember, the cost of living increases approximately 3-5% each year! Your savings will always be severely capped if you view earning money from the perspective of having only one stream of income. If you have several streams of income, your ability to save money can double or expand beyond doubling.

In addition to receiving better compensation for the hours they expend in exchange for building wealth, entrepreneurs are rewarded with the knowledge that they are in control of securing their future, rather than working to secure the company's future. They are not wondering whether their job will be there each month in order to earn a paycheck. It's very hard to put a dollar amount on that type of security.

In exchange for the time they invest, Motivated entrepreneurs gain an indescribable sense of accomplishment with what they have done for themselves and their family. They have the pride of knowing that they are building wealth, which will be an inheritance blessing for their children and grandchildren, long after they have left this earth. Having such a worthwhile sense of accomplishment certainly contributes to a happy, well-lived life.

8. Manage Fear

When a person gives fear free reign in their life, it can stop a Motivated person in their tracks quicker and more permanently than anything else. Fear can cause even the most diligent entrepreneur to become overwhelmed and paralyzed to the point that they abandon their path and run back to their old comfort zone. When fear rears its ugly head, a mindset shift can mean the difference between continuing on, or stopping your Motivated life journey. Fear is a force that must be reckoned with in the entrepreneur's life, and you cannot let it take control and win in your life.

To create a mindset shift, you must first identify your fear. What do you fear? Unfortunately, fear can appear at any time on the Motivated path. Fear is part of the human experience, but like any human experience, you must learn to manage it so that it doesn't manage you. Most entrepreneurs have one or more of the following fears during the early stages of their new Motivated life:

- **Fear of failure**. Anytime you do something that you haven't done before, there is an element of uncertainty. Uncertainty can quickly turn into fear without you realizing that it's even happening. You might see your confidence in achieving success quickly morph into a fear of failure. That's when you need a mindset shift.

    Rather than concentrating on the fact that you could fail, start thinking about how you could succeed. Give yourself pep talks to get your mind in the mode of thinking success. What will your reward be when you succeed? You'll enjoy a sense of accomplishment. You'll benefit financially and be able to provide you and your family with a keener sense of security and the lifestyle that you desire. You've been courageous to manage your finances in such a way that you can leave an inheritance for your children and grandchildren. And, the list of benefits for your success goes on and on.

- Fear that the product, business, service, course, system, book, etc. are not ready to launch. Launching your business can certainly bring on cold feet and make you want to run away like a runaway bride at the altar on her wedding day. Just like the runaway bride who can't muster the courage to face her forever partner at the altar, you might find yourself willing to forsake everything that you have invested in your business just to avoid facing the fear of the launch. This type of fear can be paralyzing, causing procrastination, delayed launch dates, mental anguish, and loss of revenue.

  If you took the time and developed the necessary skill set to do your best work, covered all of the important bases, sought the advice and opinions of experts and have given everything needed to pour into your business, then you are ready. Instead of letting that worrisome nagging voice convince you that you're not ready, you need to develop the mindset that your business is great, serves a purpose in your life and in the lives of others. You need to convince yourself that you must launch your business and not delay the launch due to your fears.

  Visualize how wonderful it will feel once the business is launched. Visualize the reward of your labor. Remind yourself that hundreds of thousands of entrepreneurs have successfully launched their business before you, and many of them were highly successful.

- **Fear of disappointing the people in your life who you care about, and who you want to take care of and impress.** Walking the Motivated path doesn't only impact you. It might affect your significant other and children in an up-close and personal way. This can be terrifying to the entrepreneur. If anything can make one run back to what they perceive as safety, knowing that their actions might actually negatively impact the ones they love is the thing to do it.

  The mindset shift that you need to embrace when you worry about how your business might negatively affect your loved ones is to remain confident in remembering that there is no safety or security for you or your family on the Misplaced path. The best thing you can do for your loved ones is to responsibly go to the next level, because by doing so, you can elevate their lives to the next level. Even if things don't work out exactly as you had intended, you are showing your children how to muster the courage to move forward even in the face of fear. This is a lesson that all children (and adults) must learn if they are to succeed in life.

- **Fear of loss.** When you have something that seems secure, it can be extremely difficult to let go of it in order to embrace something else, even when you perceive that something else as better. (Remember the little boy holding the balloons and lollipops, unable to let go to accept the bigger prize!) Sometimes, it's necessary to transition slowly and let go of your former job or income in increments in order to ensure that you are being responsible in taking care of your family, paying your bills, etc. Be patient with that process, but don't give up on the process. Develop the mindset that you can't lose what you don't have—and remember that remaining on the Misplaced path does not give you what you need for sustaining a prosperous, happy life.

- **Fear of not doing things "right."** Too many people believe that there is only one proper way to do something. This close-minded view destroys creativity. Rather than fretting over whether you are doing everything just right, according to whoever tells you what the right way is, broaden your mind to explore what you are doing, and do it well according to what seems right to you. Will you make mistakes? Of course, you will. The person who tells you how to do it "right" made mistakes too. They made mistakes that enabled them to keep improving their "right," and so will you. Every mistake you make will actually help make your business better. Don't worry about perfection. Your focus should not be on achieving perfection; your focus is on making progress.

- **Fear of being ridiculed by family, friends, peers, and those in your industry**. The entrepreneur who succumbs to the fear of ridicule by others will never enjoy success because they will always do things to avoid being ridiculed rather than taking steps to move forward. They'll constantly question whether what they are doing will result in them being mocked or put down. This is a huge burden to carry on your shoulders, and it's one that you should not accept because it serves no good purpose on the Motivated path. The entrepreneur must be thick-skinned. They have developed the mindset that they are taking care of their business and if others don't approve, it's their problem, not the entrepreneur's. You don't have time for such immature drama and peer pressure. You are too busy developing yourself and your brand, and realizing your dreams, to stop and listen to the clatter that could discourage you.

Many successful entrepreneurs have gone before you, paving the way like brave and heroic pioneers. There has never been a better time to be an entrepreneur. Develop the entrepreneur mindset. Utilize it in every area of your life, and you'll see self-improvement.

Motivated Thinking from Chapter 11:

- You must develop an entrepreneurial mindset if you want to live the Motivated life.
- Thinking like an entrepreneur in all areas of your life will serve you well on your path to future success.

Chapter 12:

Step 5

Own Your Financial Future

"You don't need to be a rocket scientist. Investing is not a game where the guy with the 160 IQ beats the guy with the 130 IQ"

~Warren Buffet.

This is likely the most important subject in this book. This chapter on finances is meant to be informative and thought provoking. However, the actual action steps that must be taken in any financial planning process are solely up to you. Nobody can make decisions for you in this area without your guidance, because only you, and you alone, know your optimal outcome, and the risk that you're willing to take along the way. This book and its author are not attempting to encourage any particular plan or type of investment, and you should either learn what is needed on your own with study beyond this chapter, or seek the help of a financial planning professional.

What this chapter can do for you is help you begin learning the key benefits of saving and investing, and provide you with a very simple plan on how to begin. If you're already an investor, this will serve as a helpful recap of the basics of financial education.

Any book that tries to help liberate you from being stuck in life, pursue a path that's based on your passion and purpose, and that leads to real freedom, CANNOT help you achieve any of those goals without addressing this immensely critical topic.

Taking control of your financial future lays the foundation for your Motivated life. This chapter merely provides an overview of what your thinking needs to be in this area. As with all financial advice, you need to seek your own advice and make your own decisions. The main goal of this chapter is to highlight the key financial topics that you should focus on as you begin to take control of your financial future. You simply cannot allow yourself to end up like most Americans, living paycheck to paycheck with little to no savings, and no peace of mind. Succeeding in all other areas of your life, while not controlling your finances isn't success at all.

In order to take control of your financial future, you need to understand the basics of savings and investing. Most people spend little to no time on this type of material. Below are some rules on how to think about managing money in your life, and then once you have it, how to make your money grow.

New research from Charles Schwab shows that three in five Americans live paycheck to paycheck, but only one in four have a written financial plan. According to Charles Schwab's 2018 Modern Wealth Index, that's because few people in the U.S. believe that their level of wealth deserves a plan.

"The idea that financial planning and wealth management are just for millionaires is one of the greatest misconceptions among Americans, and one of the most damaging," says Joe Vietri, a senior vice president and Head of Schwab's retail branch network.

Most Americans know that they need a financial plan but according to the study, the majority don't have a plan due to the following reasons:

- **They don't feel that they have enough money to need a plan;**
- **They wouldn't know how to make a plan; and**
- **They don't think that they can stick to a plan if they had one.**

Let's make this point abundantly clear. If you're not 100% in control of your finances, and have a written plan that you're following, then you're not in control of your life. It's as basic as that! When you aren't in control of your finances, you have essentially turned over one of the most important areas of your life to someone else. Worse yet, it means that there is no captain of your ship in this crucial area, and it is all left simply to chance.

Did you know that in the richest and most prosperous country in the world, the average American can't afford to handle a $500 emergency? How is that possible? How is it that in such an advanced society, the vast majority of people know next to nothing about financial planning and investing? One of the main reasons is that money management and investing is not taught in schools. Another reason is that most parents don't have the requisite knowledge themselves, they are therefore, incapable of teaching their children about the importance of saving and investing. As with any other uncomfortable topic, if we try to avoid addressing it, we easily can. At the end of the day, without some proactive effort on your part, what you learn in the financial area comes largely from a few brief conversations with those closest to you. So, unless you come from a family of millionaires, or have financially savvy parents, you likely have a significant amount of work to do in this critical area.

Did you ever wonder why simple principles of money like compound interest aren't taught in elementary school? Why isn't the notion of saving and investing routinely taught to students? Why aren't more parents more concerned with teaching children and teens about managing their money and investing? If elementary and high school students were taught about money matters and investing, there would be vastly more adults with financial freedom well before and into their retirement years. Today, many young adults struggle financially well into their college years, only to live the next few decades financially frustrated while they pay off their student loans. How many parents do you personally know who have their college graduates living with them? The next generation may be the first downwardly mobile generation. Why?

The majority of people who came from families without excess money started out just like you. They earned at least one degree and incurred significant debt along the way. They took a job in order to get their foot in the door somewhere, and they worked hard. Many times, they sacrificed their own self-worth to please others, all with the hope that they would advance and one day get... what? Freedom and control! But for most of them, it's merely an illusion. By the time they reach this realization, and truly comprehend its implications, they are trapped. They have incurred far too much debt to start over. They bought a lifestyle, not a life. And for that, they will pay a huge price.

Do you know anyone who hates their career or is stuck in a dead-end job, largely because they can't afford to make a change? It's one of the worst and most uncomfortable positions to be in, but it's a situation that's utterly predictable the moment that you enter the Misplaced path. And yet, with a few simple strategies, it can all turn out completely different. Most people wish late in life that someone would have taken the time to teach them about finances and investing early in life. Well, it's never too late to learn. If you start today by understanding the basics of investing, you will be on your way to financial peace of mind.

Investing

Unfortunately, the subject of investing is often viewed as too daunting and difficult for the average person. The reality is that investing has never been simpler to learn and do than it is today. How to invest in your financial future is greatly misunderstood. Many people think that simply because they don't have the education, sophistication, or knowledge to invest, they shouldn't do it. Why? Because it's easier to stand still and not learn, even if that results in leading an unhappy and unfulfilling life! Those people won't start educating themselves on how to invest even if it means that without additional income, they will have to continue working two or more jobs just to make ends meet. Despite the fact that there are scores of great books teaching everyday people how to invest and become successful at it, very few people actually invest at all, and even fewer do it well.

"Motivated or Misplaced" is a book about the path that you're on across many important areas of your life, and how to create change if you have the courage to try. So, let's start by looking more closely at saving and investing, which can be a significant part of being on the Motivated path.

What You Risk by Not Understanding Investing

Sometimes the best way to truly understand the value of something is to realize what you're missing by not having it. If you don't understand financial planning and investing, then here's just a short list of the consequences. The price that you pay for not being financially educated includes:

Lack of Control	You aren't in control of your future. Circumstances will overtake you and you won't have any feeling of confidence.
Fear	You worry about everything--bills, how you're going to balance everything with the limited amount of money you make, and the

	reality that any small unplanned financial event can throw you into full panic mode.
Low Self-Esteem	You are unable to feel good about yourself and your life unless you are in control of your finances.
Frustration	Are you tired of not being able to afford the things that you want?
No Peace of Mind	There is no true peace of mind when you know that your finances are a mess.

Now, if somebody told you that they could teach you something that could significantly improve your feeling of control, reduce your fears, improve your self-esteem and give you peace of mind, would you be willing to listen and learn? Then, welcome to the world of financial planning and investing! From this day forward, this will be a mindset that you will be conscious of every day. Unlike most authors covering this subject, this book is not about naming all of the sacrifices you will need to make in order to be a successful investor. The goal of every area of this book is to get you to take action and to get started on your new path. Starting to take action is always the hardest part. However, action leads to momentum, which leads to results. Momentum will come, once action is consistent.

Before we explore any of the financial planning ideas that you can use to take control of your finances, let's talk about a few high-level principles that are important to live by. They include:

- **Spend less than you make**. Establish a budget that covers your expenses and allows you to save at least 10% of your monthly income for investing. Stick to the budget and invest intelligently, after paying off any high interest debts. This seems so simple, but so many people fail to follow this basic concept. Alternatively, spending everything you earn, or worse, yet, spending money you haven't earned yet, will lead to a disastrous financial situation. Believe it or not, having material possessions will not bring happiness. If you think it does, seek help and get to the root of your desire which is likely to fill some emotional need. Having stuff is simply having stuff. There is nothing wrong with having things that you enjoy and use. However, there is something amiss when you must have things just to make you feel good. Buy what you need and what you really want, but stop spending money on things that don't really matter for more than five minutes.

- **Avoid long-term credit card debt.** Most Americans carry a lot of debt, particularly credit card debt. Credit cards have a place and can serve you well under certain conditions, but in many cases, people abuse credit cards. They consider them as "available money" for purchases that the person can't reasonably afford to buy with cash. When a credit card bill isn't paid in full each month, the balance rises quickly, due to the high interest on unpaid purchases. Very quickly, the credit card holder becomes indebted for several thousand dollars. According to Magnify Money, Americans who carry credit card debt from month-to-month have an average credit card balance of $4,453 and pay over $1,100 per year in interest alone on that credit card debt (Magnify Money 2018). That $1,100 could be used for investments rather than merely wasting it on useless credit card interest payments.

    If you are to become financially free to invest, you must understand that a credit card is not money for you to use as though it is cash in your wallet. Rather, it is credit that you can access. It is money that you do not have, but can borrow. This money costs you money, in the form of interest. This should be avoided whenever possible!

- **Have specific goals for your money**. Instead of being passive with your money, put it to work for you by investing in assets. If you do not invest your money, it is not working for you. Those who build wealth make their money work for them. Determine how you will make your money work for you! Do your homework, and know which investments are right for your specific situation. Create a plan for when and how you will invest your money.

    Avoid acquiring unnecessary liabilities. Before making purchases, ask yourself what your purchase will truly cost you. What will it cost in interest if you buy the item on credit? What will it cost each month or year to store it, insure it, and maintain it? When it becomes obsolete or no longer works, what will it take to dispose of the item?

As an example, you may want to buy a new car. You check out the financing on the car you want and find that the payments are $380 per month. Let's assume that amount fits within your budget for a new car. But as you keep researching all of the cars' related costs, you find out that the insurance is off the charts because of the way the car is categorized. You check further and find out the gas mileage isn't great. What will you spend each month in insurance and gasoline? All of these expenses are directly related to owning a new vehicle. If you're able and willing to spend the full amount for the vehicle and maintenance, then it works. Just be aware that your new car is not only going to cost $480 per month. Be realistic about each of your liabilities.

Take the time to determine whether you really need the item you want to buy. In America, there is a warped sense of what we "need." Many people who visit or go to work and live in other countries often come back to the United States with a changed view of what they actually need. Perhaps, most of us would benefit from spending time in a third-world country where the people need water, food, and shelter from the elements, rather than a garage and storage unit full of unappreciated and unused "toys" and items purchased from a "keeping up with the Joneses" attitude. Most families in European countries live in homes significantly smaller than ours and are perfectly content. In fact, there are many studies indicating the increased happiness in countries whose citizens that have less things!

The more money you spend on things, the less money you have for investing. You should adopt the mindset now not to throw away investable money on things that don't really matter to you.

- **Create multiple streams of income so that you're not over reliant on any one source.** You have no idea what the near future may bring. Even when something seems like a sure thing, it might not be. If you have not set up and managed your finances, and are still depending on only that one seemingly sure stream of income, you are at significant risk of that stream drying up. It will take education, creative thinking and valuable time to set up multiple streams of income, but doing so can be a financial lifesaver.

What types of income streams should you pursue? If you are new to investing, you will be surprised by how many options are out there. Obviously, you want to choose streams of income that are feasible for you and fit both your overall financial plan, and risk tolerance for building wealth. Income may be generated across a number of diversified investments such as stocks, dividends, investment properties, investments in a business, online sales of information products including books or educational courses, high-yield savings accounts, and income from a lucrative hobby. You and you alone will have to decide what investments work best in your situation.

- **Be persistent.** Investments don't always turn out the way that you plan. Don't despair and give up during those times, and don't let a setback scare you away from investing. Keep investing wisely. Keep learning. Investments are not meant to provide instant wealth but rather a steady building block of wealth. Look at the long-term, big picture rather than the short-term setback.

   If you have a short-term setback, don't let that scare send you back to safety. Part of living the Motivated life is not being intimidated by others and being confident with your own decisions. Be persistent, do your studying, and let your good decisions play out. In the long- term, you'll be glad that you did.

- **Continue learning from those who have mastered investing.** Never assume that you know enough about investing. Investing changes. The market changes. You can never know enough about investing. Learn the basics and build on it constantly. Stay current with the latest investment news. Also, continue to learn from mentors, financial coaches, and other experts in this area. Schedule time for listening to podcasts, reading books, watching reputable YouTube videos, taking online classes, and attending seminars. Several top investing books and financial planning apps are listed at the end of this book to help.

- **Focus on ideas, not on things**. Instead of trying to figure out the perfect product to sell, focus on concepts and life-changing strategies that can change your life and the life of others. Building wealth goes beyond simply finding the perfect material product to "make you rich." In fact, that kind of thinking can be detrimental to your financial future, as it is limiting and, to some extent, without purpose. Invest in concepts and strategies that can change lives, enrich others, and accomplish your business goals. These investments are extremely valuable in many ways. You have unique ideas and strategies that only you can bring forth, so don't be afraid to develop them.

- **Be open-minded**. Money is not the only thing you can invest. Invest in the growth and development of your personal life, significant other, children, extended family, friends, and those in your community. Invest in your spiritual life. Invest in your health. All of these things are worthy of your time and effort. Investing in all of these things will bring good results that lead to a successful, Motivated life.

Financial investments come in many forms and it's important to understand which ones are right for you. Below are the top investment options, briefly defined. You will need to decide which are best for you.

INVESTMENT	OVERVIEW
STOCKS	Also known as an equity or a share, a stock gives you a stake in a company. Basically, you get partial ownership of a public company. If you're relatively young, stocks should comprise a large percentage of your portfolio. In addition to owning a stake in a company, some stocks pay dividends, which are monthly or quarterly payments based upon your ownership, further enhancing your potential gains.
BONDS	"Bond" is a broad term that includes any type of debt investment. When you buy a bond, you loan money to an entity (a corporation or the government, for example), and they pay you back over a set period of time with a fixed interest rate. Your

investment plan must include a certain percentage of bonds.

REAL ESTATE

According to Investopedia, any real estate you buy and then rent out or resell is an ownership investment. This type of investment often includes rental homes and apartment units.

PRECIOUS METALS

Precious metals, art, collectables, *etc.* are considered an ownership-type of investment if the intention is to resell them for a profit.

MUTUAL FUNDS

Basically, a mutual fund is another term for an investment fund. Investopedia describes it as follows:

An investment vehicle that is made up of a pool of funds collected from many investors for the purpose of investing in securities such as stocks, bonds, money market instruments and similar assets. Mutual funds are operated by money managers, who invest the fund's capital and attempt to produce capital gains and income for the fund's investors. A mutual fund's portfolio is structured and maintained to match the investment objectives stated in its prospectus.

INDEX FUNDS

An index fund is a type of mutual fund with a portfolio constructed to match or track the components of a market index, such as the Standard & Poor's 500 Index (S&P 500). An index mutual fund is said to provide broad market exposure, low operating expenses and low portfolio turnover.

ETF	An ETF, or exchange-traded fund, is a marketable security that tracks an index, a commodity, bonds, or a basket of assets like an index fund. Unlike mutual funds, an ETF trades like a common stock on a stock exchange. ETFs experience price changes throughout the day as they are bought and sold.
REIT	Real Estate Investment Trusts, or REITs, are another way to invest in real estate. Instead of buying property, you invest in a company that owns and manages real estate investments.
COMMODITIES	Investing in a commodity is investing in resources that impact the economy. Oil, beef and coffee beans are all different types of commodities. The contracts you use to buy these goods are called Futures Contracts, and you buy them through a National Futures Association broker.
BUSINESSES	Starting your own business—a product or service meant to earn a profit— is another type of investment.
CD	A CD, or certificate of deposit, is a note issued by a bank in exchange for your money. You commit to leaving your money in the account for a set period in exchange for a low interest return.

Each of these brings its own level of risk and return, and you should study a lot more about them before putting any of your money into these options. Even so, below is a simple way of setting up your initial investment plan as a way to begin.

How to Begin: One simple plan to help with the discipline of investing

Living a Motivated life is about taking action, and that must include your finances. The sooner you improve this area of your life, the sooner you will see results in many other areas as well.

So, how do you begin to invest? First and foremost, you should either learn a lot more on your own, or seek advice from a professional before making any financial steps based on the sample plan below. This is a simplified version of how to organize your investments, once you have them. This is in no way a substitute for your own financial plan developed by you alone, or with the help of a financial planning professional. This is meant for illustrative purposes only.

For this portion of the book, let's assume that you have structured your life in such a way that you are ready to invest. That is, you designed your circumstances in such a way that you spend less than you earn, and have money available to invest. It also means that you don't have any high interest credit card debt eating away at your net worth while you are trying to invest. Having these things in order sets the foundation for investing.

There are four key areas of focus in the plan:

1) Debt
2) Security
3) Growth
4) Fun

How much that you choose to invest in each one of these areas is ultimately up to you, and is a result of your current status, age, career, risk tolerance, and other factors. You will have to create your own plan either alone or with help from others. Either way, you will end up focusing on these four areas.

Let's look at each of these areas more closely.

DEBT	• Mortgages • Short Term Debt • Credit Cards • Car Loans • Personal Loans • Anything with Financing

Your Goal: Only use when necessary, keep balances at or near zero.

Unless you're a sophisticated investor who knows how to use debt effectively, you should have as little as possible in your life. It's usually a worthy goal to have no debt. However, if you carry a low interest mortgage on your home for example, paying that off early rather than investing the money in higher rate security or growth assets is not an ideal move.

You would be better off spending the extra money on an investment that earns a higher level of interest rather than using it to pay off a mortgage with a lower interest rate. High interest credit card debt should be avoided at all cost and any debt that you have in this area must be <u>entirely eliminated first before taking any further steps under your financial plan</u>. If you are making 10% on your investments yearly, and are paying 28% on a credit card, it makes no sense to make that investment. It is crucial that you full comprehend this principle before you embark upon any investment strategy.

SECURITY	• 3-6 Months Cash Reserves • Fixed Income Investments • Bonds • Gold / Silver • Insurance • 401K • Home

Your Goal: Investments with a guaranteed rate of return over time. These are relatively safe investments and should make up a significant portion of your savings.

Investing in your Security is about two things: 1) Providing you with long term peace of mind; and 2) Helping you take advantage of compound interest. Both are very important in your life if you're going to have a Motivated life when it comes to money. These investments aren't based on the latest hot stock tips, or high growth start-up. Those are discussed in the Growth area. Security is your foundation and until you have this, you do not have the foundation to invest in higher risk Growth investments. Most experts would suggest keeping 30-40% of your investments in this area, but this largely depends upon your age. If you're in the early stages of your career, you can afford to put more of your investment money into Growth areas. However, that is solely up to you.

GROWTH
- Mutual Funds
- Stocks
- Real Estate
- Stock Options
- Cryptocurrencies
- Business Ventures

Your Goal: These investments are riskier but also might provide a higher rate-of-return. These should make up the majority of what you save until late in life when any type of loss cannot be sustained.

These are considered your unlimited risk investment instruments, but they can also provide unlimited rewards.

After you've addressed the debt in your life and have funded your Security investments, you can begin to take on more risk and look to higher growth investments. Picking stocks might seem very time-consuming, but the way to look at it for the long-term is that you are buying into a business. You want to think like an owner when buying stocks, and not like a trader. Unless you are going to spend a lot of your time researching companies, the best thing that you can do is buy into a mutual fund that will perform at least as well as the overall market. Keep in mind that over 90% of mutual funds don't beat the market in terms of their performance. When you then take out the associated fees (which varies greatly, so you need to perform due diligence here too) charged by the company managing the mutual fund, you are even further behind than the market.

The easiest way to track the market, and outperform most mutual funds and individual investors over time, is to buy into a Stock Market Index Fund. According to Mark Waldman, investment advisor and former finance professor at American University, the data is very clear and shows that over any period of time longer than, say, ten years, the S&P 500 index funds outperform all other kinds of mutual funds. This is a great starting place for you.

If you pay off your high interest debt, adequately fund your security plan, and buy into an index fund, your financial profile and plan will be miles ahead of most people in the United States. You'll be on a path to having financial abundance long-term which will allow you to pursue your passions with fun and excitement.

FUN	• Vacations • Trips • Toys • Experiences

Your Goal: Invest in things that help you enjoy your life.

Speaking of fun and excitement, the final area of your plan is to create a Fun plan. This is your reward for having the determination to address the three previous core areas. What you put into this fund and how you spend it is all up to you – you've earned it!

Earning a financial education and creating an investment plan can seem like very daunting task, and even though what's been outlined here is a very basic approach, it is one that will serve you well and allow you to focus on other areas of your life with greater confidence.

If you do nothing more than pay off high interest debts, invest in an Index Fund and buy bonds yearly to diversify, you would already be ahead of the majority of people in America!

Investing in your own financial future is a critical component of the Motivated life. You can't pursue your dreams and live your purpose and passion if you can't take care of your family and obligations. As stated before, but is worth repeating, the most important point here is that you have a plan. Have a plan and initiate it as early in your life as possible. The younger you are when you start investing, the far better off you will be. Do not put it off as something you will do when you feel better prepared to do it. Do it as soon as you can.

If you'd like to delve further in the area of financial planning and investing, I've included a list of additional books and planning applications at the conclusion of the book. Two books to start with are: 1) Rich Dad, Poor Dad, by Robert Kiyosaki, which is an excellent book to help understand the philosophy of creating wealth, and 2) Money: Master The Game, by Tony Robbins. Tony's book takes you through specific and time-tested principles of how to invest for the long term, and take total control of your financial life.

This is an area of your life that will reward you handsomely for putting in the time to learn what to, and what not to do, with your wealth. You must be 100% responsible and in control of this area for you to truly live a Motivated life.

Motivated Thinking from Chapter 12:

- There is nothing mysterious or difficult about investing.
- Get your finances in order so you have money to invest.
- Start investing as soon as you can, but live your life and let your investments pay off over the long-term.
- Only you are responsible for your money, and the advice in this book is only meant to provide you with an example of a path to consider.

Chapter 13

Step 6

Embrace Change

"The secret of change is to focus all of your energy, not on fighting the old, but on building the new."

~ Socrates

In his article in Psychology Today titled, "Adapting to Change," Barton Goldsmith, Ph.D., states the following about change:

"Things change constantly. Loved ones die; jobs end, as do relationships. People get promoted, couples bond in marriage and babies are born. Guess what? The positive changes can be as hard to adapt to as the negative ones."

Mr. Goldsmith offers the following tips on adjusting to change:

- "When a good change appears, accept it with grace. You may not believe you deserve it, or you just may not be ready for it, but the only way to move forward and get the most out of it is to embrace the positivity, however it shows up."

- "When a negative change is looming, start looking for alternatives before it actually happens, if you can. For example, if you know your company is in trouble and you are hearing things that are making you insecure, don't wait to get laid off, but start looking for another job. Even if your current position isn't changed, you will have gained valuable experience and maybe a better gig."

Adapting to change is vital to our view and experience of the future.

"Our only security is our ability to change."

~ John Lilly

Whether you've been on the path of the Motivated life for a short while or for several years now, you've learned that success is a journey, not a destination. You don't ever fully arrive. Instead, you continuously evolve, one day at a time, for the remainder of your life on this earth. You evolve by getting up every single morning with a determination in your heart to be the best you that you are capable of being right now. You have faith in yourself to take the next step to be where you need to be next. You continue your journey with the confidence that you are using your time wisely today to accomplish that which allows you to continue to be free and unencumbered by someone else's idea and plan for your life. You have the courage to live your authentic life every day; the one you were meant to live.

It wouldn't be fair to talk about your journey to success without also mentioning that you will sometimes end up on the wrong path as you walk forward. Even with a focused ambitious effort, you will sometimes, perhaps even often, find yourself on the wrong path. You are human, and humans cannot walk a perfect journey without making mistakes, becoming involved in circumstances that lead to detours, and experiencing times when things just don't work out the way you want. You have a physical body to contend with, other people to live in unity with, and the daily pressures that living in our society places on your shoulders—particularly if you're not careful to avoid these pressures as much as possible.

There might be many distractions along the journey. You might view some of these distractions as huge things, events or people. You will only learn, often too late, that the best things, events, and people will walk with you on your journey rather than insist that you come off your path and join theirs. You'll learn that some distractions are necessary in order for you to be the best caring, giving person that you can. Sometimes, you'll choose, with love, to get off your path for a short time so that you can put your arms around someone who needs your full attention for just a while.

Pitfalls that you don't see coming may ground you temporarily, making you feel as though your fantastic journey of success has ended. Wrong thinking can appear on the doorstep of your mind and beg to restore itself in the apartment of your brain. But you know how to get off the ground, wipe the dust from your clothes and march on with the peace and joy that you've come to know and cherish while living the Motivated life.

There might be life changes over which you have no control, that may cause you to reconsider and change the direction you are going. Your journey of success is not a streamlined, direct path from A to Z. Life doesn't work that way, no matter how well you plan or execute your plan. Part of living the open-minded Motivated life is having the wisdom to know what you can control and what you can't control, and making necessary adjustments as needed. You have to be adaptable and flexible when you are confronted with unanticipated circumstances. You must take action and not give into fears.

Whether it's in your physical life, professional life, or personal life, you will find yourself heading in the wrong direction from time to time. This is not a sign of failure or weakness. It doesn't mean you've done something wrong. It simply means that it's time to stop and examine where you are and how you are positioned to continue. Here are some questions you can ask yourself to help you determine what's next:

- Do you still have a vision for the Motivated life?
- Are you still visualizing the next stage of your life?
- Are you currently pointed in the proper direction in order to end up where you want to end up?
- Did you miss a turn or a step somewhere along the way and need to back-track to pick up what you missed?
- Have you taken on habits that are sabotaging your Motivated life?
- Who is influencing you? Are they affecting your ability to live a Motivated life? Have you allowed naysayers, toxic people, or those who undermine and sabotage your efforts back into your life?
- When you were climbing over one of the mountains, did you come down on the wrong side and need to go back over the mountain?
- Does the way you expend your time, energy, and resources contribute to your journey?
- Do you still feel the passion in your heart to live a free and Motivated life?
- What has changed since you began your journey to success? And, what effect did those changes have on your journey?
- Do you still desire to use your skills and talents to make your Motivated life a continued reality?

Every day, you have the option to go another way and live a Misplaced life - a life that someone else has chosen for you; a life without the freedom to pursue your dreams. When you are weary and can't see the next step ahead, you might be sorely tempted to run back to the path that is familiar. Each day, the decision is yours. You can give up on your Motivated life or you can get back on the right path and give it everything you've got to continue to it. The key to continue living the Motivated life is to understand how to get back on the right path and to excel once you do. If you must, wallow in self-pity for a moment—but only for a moment. Or two. Wipe away the tears, stand up, and figure out how to move forward.

Don't Overthink

There's a famous speech online titled "Just Do It," that was given many years ago by a very successful football coach and businessman named Art Williams. That was before Nike chose those words for their slogan. The speech is electrifying because in it, Art takes the concept of success, which many people turn into a very complicated subject, and boils it down into the simple concept of don't think too much, "Just Do It!"

People overthink things for a variety of reasons. Some just want to make sure they get it right. They are obsessed with having every detail worked out before they take one step forward. They replay every scenario in their head and repeat everything that might go wrong over and over in their mind. Rather than think about what might go right, they dwell on what could possibly go wrong. Of course, you should think things through and try to prevent making costly and time-consuming mistakes. You should make sure that what you are going to do is in your best interest and won't be harmful to anyone else. But, don't dwell on all of the things that might go wrong. Think about a positive outcome. Visualize how wonderful it will feel to accomplish the step or goal.

Overthinking can be a way of procrastinating so that you get out of doing something that you want to do, but are afraid to start, or believe that you don't know how. In that instance, when you continue thinking about the thing that you want to do instead of acting on it, you continue putting off taking any steps. The mindset to adopt is, instead of overthinking, make it simple—find a way to boost your confidence to move forward. Seek out the advice of a positive mentor; research the topic; take a class and learn more about what you're going to do. Do something and take some action because you must gain the confidence required to do what you need to do. Take a step.

Overthinking can turn a simple task or step into a monumental, complicated task or step. Making something far more complicated than it really is causes some people to feel justified in taking far too long to complete the step or task. They have a pat answer for when others ask how the task is coming along - "It's complicated."

If you subconsciously want to sabotage your goal, overthinking might be the perfect ticket. If you think about it long enough, the opportunity disappears, or the timing is so far off that it's no longer feasible to move forward. Then, you're off the hook—off the hook for finding the freedom to control your own life. It's not worth it! Don't sabotage your steps and goals. Roll up your sleeves and get to work. There simply is no room for sabotage on the Motivated path.

In business and in life, the people who reach success, as defined by them, are those who don't overthink things, they just do it. Do what? Whatever it takes to reach their goals. If you're committed to living the Motivated life it won't be easy, but it's simple and it's absolutely worth it.

Focus on the End Results

The easy path will always present itself to you, especially when uncertainty plagues you. Your mind will play tricks on you and make it appear like the easy way is the obvious option. That doesn't mean it's the path you should take.

The easy path might be tempting when you are weary and aren't seeing the results as soon as you had hoped. This happened to Emily when she was on her successful journey to a healthy body and weight loss to provide her with the energy needed to fulfill her duties at her new business. During her first two months on the eating plan, Emily saw a terrific weight loss of 25 pounds. Then, the weight loss stopped. The numbers on the scale did not budge no matter what Emily did. Emily became weary because she wasn't seeing results right then. She wanted to believe that the weight loss plan wouldn't work for her, and that she should just give up.

However, she stayed the course and kept on taking care of herself. She continued seeking advice from others who had used the plan. She surrounded herself with supportive people who cared about her success. Emily had the courage to ignore the temporary stall and instead, looked toward the end goal of being at a healthy weight by the end of the year. Even though she saw no weight loss for two entire months, the following month the scale indicated that she had lost fifteen pounds. She continued to lose more weight and ended up meeting her final goal by the end of the year.

It's no different with self-development, business, or finances. You must be steadfast in your mission. During those times when all seems lost, focus on your end result. Stay the course. Don't quit, don't give in, and for the love of God, don't take advice from those who do. It's always puzzling when people who have given up on their own goals and dreams, find it easy to give advice to others. Even more confusing is why anyone would deem such an advisor as worthy of following. Instead, pay attention and copy those who have hiked the mountain before you, those who understood the difficulty in making decisions but persevered and succeeded.

Say No to Naysayers and Drama

When certain people see you pulling away and making a concerted effort to live life on your terms, they will discourage you, encourage you to take the easy path, and commiserate with you when things don't work out. They may say things to you such as, "Don't put yourself through that; take the easy path." "Why bother with that when you could live a life that is easier?" "Why can't you just settle for doing things the way everyone else does them?"

They see life through their own lenses and insecurities and are happy to put their views onto you. When you have the courage to pursue your dreams, even though it's not easy, doing so might remind those naysayers of how unwilling they are to pursue their own dreams. If you accept what is disguised as caring and support, that is tantamount to taking directional advice from a tourist. They don't know, and they can't help. They are not you and do not have your vision. They don't have the fire burning inside of them that you have burning inside of you that desires accomplishing something wonderful in your life. They don't have the "Entrepreneurial Mindset" that gives them the tools to manage their life in a way that frees them from the control of others. They don't have a passion to succeed, but you do. You have the "Entrepreneurial Mindset!" You, unlike them, want to live the Motivated life.

Even worse than the naysayers are people who are not happy unless they are creating drama everywhere they go, with everyone they know. They might be a co-worker, business partner, neighbor, someone in your social group, or a family member. They might even be your significant other! Like the cloud of dirt that follows Pig Pen in the Charlie Brown cartoons, a cloud of drama always follows some people. Drama can be a major distraction, causing you to lend your mind and efforts to a situation that is not worthy. It's best to label drama for what it is and not participate. Not participating might ultimately mean finding a way to completely avoid the person who constantly stirs up drama.

Get out of the Rut and Gain a New Perspective

As you know from an earlier chapter in this book, routine can be a creativity killer. Without the creativity to stay on your Motivated path, you might wander aimlessly and take a wrong turn, or worse yet, stand still in the same spot. We know too well that it's easy to fall into a rut and stay there, doing the same thing over and over, without realizing that progress has slowed or stopped. You have to recognize when that is happening and use your tools to dig out of that rut and go to the next level.

Your sharp perspective can become faded over time. You are not the person you were when you started your journey. You've changed, and your perspective on many things may have changed. Go to the mountaintop where the view is great, and you can gain a clear, fresh perspective. Your "mountaintop" might be a literal get-away to a quiet place so that you have time to meditate, pray, and think without the distractions of others' voices clamoring in the background. Your mountaintop might mean mapping out some new strategies to help you see things clearly. It may be a session with your coach or having a long phone call with your mentor.

It also might mean that it is the right time to have some fresh faces in your life. Spend time with new social circles that are different from your usual circle of friends. Network at new business organizations, perhaps some that are unrelated to organizations with which you are normally associated. Make new friends who are interesting, and who tell you stories that you have not heard before. New conversations can spark new ideas and cause you to seek new information.

Get Out Your Vision Board or Make a New Vision Board

Remember the vision board that you made early on when you started the journey to your Motivated life? It's time to revisit it and let it speak to you. Or, it might even be time to create a new vision board, or an additional one. Vision boards spark your emotions, motivate you, and remind you of where you are going. Also, don't forget to continue writing in your journal. These two things are not time-wasters. They help solidify your vision and keep you inspired and motivated.

Practice Gratitude for How Far You've Come

Never underestimate the power of gratitude in your life as a way to help you find your way back to the Motivated path. Gratitude is the superpower that can change your perspective, heal your heart, chase away fear, bitterness, and anger, and guide you to be the best self that you can be. Every day, give thanks for how far you've come on your Motivated path. Give thanks that you've survived every single obstacle thus far, and for having the courage to keep moving forward.

Writing in a gratitude journal is therapeutic and can help you see where you have been, what you have accomplished, and where you want to go next. It's amazing how small your problems seem when you are writing about the things for which you are thankful. The problems disappear, and opportunities appear.

Nurture Yourself

No one can go for long periods of time without taking care of themselves. When you fail to nurture yourself, you can easily fall prey to the negative thinking that makes you vulnerable to making bad decisions. Examples of this are when you allow negative people into your life, and when you expend time and energy on things that do not line up with your Motivated life. When you aren't securely on your path, it's the worst time (not that there ever is ever a good time) for making bad decisions. Eat healthy foods, at least most of the time. Exercise to stay in shape and to relieve the stresses of daily life. Get enough sleep at night, even if it means closing the laptop before you finished all of your work. Cultivate good relationships and enjoy the people with which you have those relationships. Do fun and exciting things that tickle your senses and cause you to feel alive. Know that if you take care of yourself, you'll find your North Star and you'll be back on your intended path in no time.

Owning the Rewards of the Motivated Life

Once you decide to live a Motivated life and pay the price that doing so entails, you're already a new person, and your life won't be the same. Following the tactics and steps to make it a reality is critical of course, but inside you've already transformed.

This "new you" exists in your mind, and what you do next is all about taking the steps to make the internal vision a reality in your external life – and you have to "Just Do It."

This is what will happen if you do:

- **Your standards will change.** Things that were acceptable in the past won't be anymore. You'll expect more of yourself and give more of yourself. You'll have the courage to be the bold new you and uphold your new standards without the paralyzing fear or doubt that causes you to shrink away.

- **You will use your mind to find solutions, and not constantly point out and define problems.** Talking about problems will no longer appeal to you. Your mind will be trained to seek solutions rather than dwell on problems. Solutions will be a natural part of who you are.

- **When you are confronted with a real problem, you will see an opportunity.** Rather than becoming fearful, you will look at those problems or setbacks as opportunities. You will have faith that you can handle the process and the outcome. Your life will be courage-based rather than fear-based.

- **You will have unbounded energy.** Moving forward and creating momentum is exhilarating and energizing. It feeds the soul and mind with positivity that energizes you. You will take care of yourself mentally, physically, and spiritually so that you will function at an optimal level.

- **You will wish the best for those around you and be the one to help them advance their own journey.** You won't fear that there isn't enough success to go around. Reaching for your dreams has made you so happy that you can't help but want to help others find their own happiness. With the gratitude that you feel for having been able to walk your Motivated path and live your Motivated life, you will reach out to others, support them, and help them gain sure footing on their path.

- **You will be sought out by others because your mindset will appear different and unique.** Your words and your life will shine in such a way that others will recognize that they want what you have. They will see that your smile is genuine, your gratitude is sincere, and your message is one that you live each day.

- **You will reach a level of happiness that you previously thought was only available to the truly successful people, because you are now successful too.** When you are living life on your own terms, have less worries and stress, and are able to take care of your loved ones, you will be able to live a happier life.

- **You will see other people making the mistakes that you used to make, and you will feel gratified in knowing how to avoid them.** You'll be amazed at the difference between your Motivated life and your Misplaced life. Every day, as you continue to walk further in the Motivated life, you'll see why you left the Misplaced life and started your journey. This will encourage you to continue to grow and prosper.

Living a Motivated life is a journey, but one that you will enjoy each step of the way.

Motivated Thinking from Chapter 13:	- The only thing in life that is constant is change. - Learn to welcome and adapt to change. - Change brings new challenges but also new opportunities.

Chapter 14

Step 7

Serve Others to Reach Success

"The best way to find yourself is to lose yourself in the service of others."

~ Mahatma Gandhi

In an article in Yes! magazine, titled "Five Reasons to serve others," writer Nipun Mehta brilliantly explains some of the many benefits that comes from serving others. They are listed here verbatim:

1. **Serve to discover abundance: the radical shift from 'me' to 'we.'**

When you serve, you discover that often the most important things you have to offer are not things at all. You start to uncover the full range of resources at your disposal – your time, presence, attention – and recognize that the ability to give stems from a state of mind and heart, a place much deeper than the material. Inspired by the possibilities this opens up in every moment, you begin to discover humble opportunities to serve – everywhere.

This process begins a shift from a me-orientation to a we-orientation. You start to look at people and situations with an eye for what you can offer them, and not vice versa. You break the tiresome tyranny of questions like "What's in it for me?" The mindset shifts from consumption to contribution. Paradoxically, when serving in this way, you are no longer operating from a space of scarcity. Your cup fills and overflows.

2. Serve to express gratitude.

When you acknowledge the fullness of your life, you can manifest a heart of service in any situation. In that sense, service doesn't start when we have something to give – it blossoms naturally when we have nothing left to take. And that is a powerful place to be. We begin to play our part – first, by becoming conscious of the offerings we receive, then by feeling gratitude for them, and finally by continuing to pay forward our gifts with a heart of joy.

Yes, external change is required for the world to progress, but when coupled with inner transformation, it can affect the world in a radically different way.

"We can do no great things – only small things with great love," maintained Mother Teresa, a woman who made a difference in the lives of millions. It's a matter of what we focus on. In other words, it's not just what we do that matters, but the inner impetus behind our action that really counts.

3. Serve to transform yourself.

Any time we practice the smallest act of service – even if it's only holding a door for somebody with a full heart that says, "May I be of use to this person?" – that kind of giving changes the deeply embedded habit of self-centeredness. In that brief moment, we experience other-centeredness. That other-centeredness relaxes the patterns of the ego, a collection of unexamined, self-oriented tendencies that subtly influence our choices. This is why no true act of service, however small, can ever really be wasted.

To serve unconditionally in this way takes practice and constant effort. But with time and sharpened awareness, we begin to brush against the potential for transformation that is embedded in every act of generosity. It's a realization that when you give, you actually receive. You begin to internalize this, not at the intellectual level but by experience.

4. Serve to honor our profound interconnection.

Over time, all of those small acts, those small moments, lead to a different state of being – a state in which service becomes increasingly effortless. And as this awareness grows, you inevitably start to perceive beyond individualistic patterns: Each small act of service is an unending ripple that synergizes with countless others.

As Rachel Naomi Remen stated, "When you help, you see life as weak. When you fix, you see life as broken. When you serve, you see life as whole." With that understanding, we begin to play our part – first, by becoming conscious of the offerings we receive, then by feeling gratitude for them, and finally by continuing to pay forward our gifts with a heart of joy. Each of us has such gifts: skills, material resources, connections, presence – everything we consider ourselves privileged to have. And when we actually start to use our gifts as tools to facilitate giving, we deepen our understanding of relationships and start to sync up with this vast "inner-net."

5. Serve to align with a natural unfolding.

When we increasingly choose to remain in that space of service, we start to see new things. The needs of the current situation become clearer, we become instruments of a greater order and consequently our actions become more effortless.

When a group of people perform this kind of service as a practice, it creates an ecosystem that holds a space, allowing value to emerge organically. All of this indirect value, the ripple effect, has space and time to add up, synergize with other ripples, and multiply into something completely unexpected.

In humble fashion, these ripples continue to seed unpredictable manifestations. Such an ecosystem can have its plans and strategies, but places more emphasis on emergent co-creation. So, a lot of the ripples will remain unseen for years; some perhaps will be the basis for a seventh-generation philanthropy. It doesn't matter, because they are unconditional gifts. What each of us can do, on a personal level, is make such small offerings of service that ultimately create the field for deeper change. The revolution starts with you and me.

> **"The only really happy people are those that have learned how to serve."**
>
> ~ Albert Schweitzer

The only way to truly reach the pinnacle of success is to take what you have learned and help others. There is no better feeling than realizing that you have accomplished something amazing, and that you have the capability to use that knowledge to help others.

Reaching out and helping other people will bring you more satisfaction in life than any other feeling that you will ever experience. If you've made it thus far, and if you've not only read but acted upon the previous chapters, then you are on your way to a peak in your life, one of many that you will experience over time. And with each one, it's important to look back and realize how far you have come and how many others you can help.

A good illustration of this took not long ago at a Tony Robbins seminar. A man stood up to discuss his goals, and Tony asked him what he would truly like to do with his life. He said that he wanted to reach financial independence (as he defined it) and that when he did, he wanted to teach others. Tony said, "No you won't." The man looked confused. Tony asked the man whether he felt that he was already financially successful and whether he thought he was on the right course. The man said that he didn't believe that he was successful, but that once he was, he would help others.

Tony asked him this question, "Do you know things today that would be helpful to people who are where you were several years ago?"

The man said, "Absolutely."

Then, Tony said, "You need to teach now."

The moral of the story is that teaching and helping others helps you with your own journey. You shouldn't wait until you think you have arrived before starting to help others. You need to do it now. It should be a natural part of what you do as a Motivated person. It helps you realize that you have a lot to give, and a lot more still to accomplish.

Another truth to the story is that if you don't develop the good habit of helping others now, it is highly unlikely that you will help others after you become more successful, when there are even more demands on your time and resources. Even though you might not yet have your feet firmly planted on the Motivated path, you still have plenty to share. Start sharing it now and let the gratitude you will feel in helping others become a natural part of the way you lead and influence others. Don't hold back! Instead, look back and help someone learn how to look up!

Winston Churchill said, "We make a living by what we get, we make a life by what we give." If you want to create true success and live a Motivated life, you must be willing to give to help others succeed. Here are some ideas that can help you help others.

- **Sincerely pay attention to people and inspire them**. When you pay attention to people, you can figure out more about them and become interested in what they do, what they have to say, what their dreams are, and how you can help them make those dreams a reality. You can understand how to inspire them. When people are inspired, it becomes easier for them to take their business to the next level.

- **Share your story and help the Misplaced get on the right path**. Reading this book helped you to understand that you were living a Misplaced life. From this book, you also learned how to leave behind your Misplaced life and start living the Motivated life. That means you have a unique story to share. It's a story that can help teach and inspire others. Don't keep your story to yourself!

- **Give without the expectation of anything in return**. It isn't truly giving when you give with the expectation of receiving something in return. That is an exchange, not giving. Determine what it is that you want to give and are able to give. Give what you have to give freely, out of the desire to help others succeed.

- **Provide guidance and feedback**. Remember your early steps of the Motivated life, when uncertainty gripped you by the throat and made it difficult for you to find your voice in your arena? Remember feeling lost and uncertain about what to do next? Remember feeling like you were a very small speck of dust in a huge universe of experts and phenomenal people who had already found success? As you may well know by now, that is normal for almost everyone who strives to be their best self and find success in life.

- **Give encouragement and cheer others on to success.** You never know when someone is so frustrated that they are contemplating giving up on their dreams and goals. Perhaps they just faced what they perceived as the final defeating issue on their journey. Maybe they have experienced a terrible setback that shook their confidence to the core and made them feel as though they must abandon their efforts. Your words of encouragement could be just the thing, at just the right time, that causes someone to continue their journey toward success. Never underestimate the power of a few well-chosen words of encouragement or handing someone a phone number and saying "I've been there."

- **Build genuine relationships**. Generally speaking, in our society, being busy is glorified for various reasons. Some people feel that being busy signifies that they are an important person who can't be bothered with mundane things and unimportant people. Some use "being too busy" as an excuse for not having to do things that they don't want to do. Many people do not understand that being busy and being productive are two different things, and they wear their being "busy" claim as though it were a badge of honor. Sadly, being busy is also used as a reason to neglect building relationships. Being too busy to build relationships is not something an influencer can afford. A leader and influencer must take the time to build genuine relationships with the people they hope to help and influence. Building relationships is essential for winning the trust of others. People do not follow leaders they do not trust.

- **Work cohesively with the team**. Motivated professionals set aside personal differences and work together for the success of each other. They demonstrate to all that everyone on the team has something of value to contribute, and they respectfully and graciously accept the contributions of others. Motivated leaders serve as the adhesive for a unified, productive team that gets results.

The Motivated life is a rich life, filled with the joy of helping others. May you always enjoy!

Motivated Thinking from Chapter 14:

- Learning to serve others ends up transforming you.
- Service to others is the pinnacle of success.
- Helping others helps you!
- There are many opportunities to serve when you look for them and remain ready and willing to help.

Chapter 15

Step 8

Internalize Perseverance

"What Defines Us is How Well We Rise After Falling."

~Anonymous

In her New York Times bestseller, "Grit," psychologist Angela Duckworth explains to anyone striving to succeed—be it parents, students, educators, athletes, or business people—that the secret to outstanding achievement is not talent but a special blend of passion and persistence she calls "grit." Duckworth, a leading researcher and professor, describes her early experiences in teaching, business consulting, and neuroscience, and how they led to her hypothesis that what really drives success is not "genius," but a unique combination of passion and long-term perseverance.

If you've followed the steps and strategies outlined in this book, your life is already on a new path – one that leads you to achieve your aspirations in life and serve as an example to those around you.

This book has been about the journey, not the arrival. If you live a Motivated life you never arrive, you constantly evolve. Life is full of challenges and changes no matter who you are, where you come from, or where you are going. You cannot just go "around" the changes that are beyond your control. The only thing you can do is successfully go through the changes.

If you have taken this book to heart, digested it, lived it, and made it a part of your emotional and intellectual being, you're now on a different journey than when you first started the book. You're now on a journey that should inevitably lead to the things that you desire and dream about, and by now, you have accomplished some of those dreams. That's an amazing thing for you, and you should be proud of your ability to remain focused and persevere through the difficult times. You should be grateful that you have found the Motivated path that has changed your life.

Unfortunately, the world is predominately made up of Misplaced people, and even after you've gotten on the Motivated path, you will still need to live and work with those who are Misplaced. You must continue to learn how to live and work without allowing the Misplaced to put their stresses and their burden of a Misplaced lifestyle onto your shoulders.

You must learn that the journey of the Misplaced is their choice. Can you show them a better path? Yes, of course. Can you lead in a way that positively influences them? Yes! Can you provide them with information, such as this book, to help them get on a better path? Absolutely. But you can't choose for them—just like no one else could have chosen the Motivated life for you. This can be frustrating, especially when it comes to loved ones and colleagues who you sincerely hope will find the path to success.

Most will not choose the Motivated life for various reasons, which were previously discussed in this book. How can you work and live in unity with those who are on a Misplaced path, while remaining firmly planted in your Motivated life?

Perseverance

Calvin Coolidge has one of the best quotes ever when it comes to being persistent.

> **"Nothing in this world can take the place of persistence. Talent will not; nothing is more common than unsuccessful people with talent. Genius will not; unrewarded genius is almost a proverb. Education will not; the world is full of educated failures. Persistence and determination alone are omnipotent."**

Remaining on the Motivated path requires perseverance. Without perseverance, you won't reach the level of success that you want, and you might find that you frequently wander back to the safety of the Misplaced life, perhaps without even realizing it. The sooner you can plant your feet firmly on the Motivated path and remain there consistently, the sooner you will realize success.

Perseverance is active and ongoing. It is an active verb meaning to remain steadfast in what you are doing, despite difficulty. You do not persevere once and then stop. You persevere every single day. In order to do that, you must truly want that thing for which you persevere.

The things that this book has asked you to focus on and do are not easy. They're simple, but not easy. There will be many times that they won't seem to be working. It will appear as though nothing is going your way, even though you have diligently tried everything that's been covered in the book. There will be days when you feel as though all of the hard work you've put in has been in vain and that you aren't any closer to your goal than when you started. In most cases, during this time, you're closer to your desired result than you have ever been! You just can't see it. It's crucial for you to find a way to keep pushing during those moments of doubt. You need to keep striving to meet the next mark if you want the benefits of your work, and if you want to see the fruition of your changed life.

Whenever you want to quit, refer back to this section of the book. Be inspired and encouraged by the many examples of people you know who have faced challenges that are most likely much larger than anything that you are up against. Remember the true stories of those people, just like you, who persevered in the face of adversity. Remember that there's almost nothing that you are trying to do, or adversity that you are facing, that has not been faced and overcome by others before you. Let those people be your inspiration, your guide, your teachers, as you continue to actively pursue the actions outlined in this book for living the Motivated life. Let the example set by these people help you continue to develop the mindset needed for perseverance.

As you study the stories of those who have persevered, make a list of the traits they share. Those who persevere develop traits that help them through the difficult times. Here are some of those traits:

- **Successful people know they must continue trying new ideas and testing their plan while they persevere.** If you've been an entrepreneur for any length of time, you have probably realized that your first idea may not necessarily be your best idea. You simply cannot know everything that you need to know, and you can't always get things right on the first, even second, third, or even fourth try. You may have to continue coming up with better ideas to drive success.

In his book, "The Tipping Point: How Little Things Can Make a Big Difference," author Malcolm Gladwell tells the story of Georgia Sadler, a nurse who wanted to bring awareness about diabetes and breast cancer to black women in the San Diego area (Gladwell, 2002). According to Gladwell's story about Sadler, the nurse set up seminars in the black churches of the city, so that women could get more information on the diseases, after they attended church. However, she noticed that even when several hundred-people attended those church services, only a few women stayed after for her free seminars.

Sadler was frustrated but realized that there must be a reason why the women weren't staying for her seminars. Her exploration of this question led her to the conclusion that the women wanted to get home after church to eat lunch and relax. She then came up with a solution. She realized that it would be best if the information were shared in a relaxed environment, and given by a speaker with whom the women were receptive to listening. Her solution was to train hair stylists to talk to women about the diseases in their beauty shops. And it worked!

- **Motivated people know that falling down and getting back up is part of their journey to success**. When they find an obstacle on their path, the Motivated person finds a way around, over, or through the boulder. They don't let other people dictate to them whether they should continue or not. They persevere. They continue. It's part of their "Entrepreneurial Mindset" and nature to keep going forward without letting anything or anyone stop them.

J.K. Rowling is an excellent example of one who persevered and became financially successful at the billionaire level. When she wrote the first Harry Potter book, she was divorced, bankrupt, and on welfare. After a dozen publishers rejected her manuscript, one finally agreed to publish it. However, that same publisher told Rowling that she needed to get a job because there was no money in children's books.

Speaking at Harvard's graduation, J.K. Rowling didn't talk about success, even though it seems she was highly qualified to do so. She spoke about failures: "You might never fail on the scale I did," Rowling told the new graduates. "But it is impossible to live without failing at something, unless you live so cautiously that you might as well not have lived at all—in which case, you fail by default." People who are highly successful, such as Rowling, know that failure is a part of success.

- **Successful people think for the long term rather than the short term.** Once when Muhammed Ali was asked if he liked training, he said that he hated training, but he told himself, "Don't quit, suffer now and live the rest of your life as a champion." When you were a child, you wanted instant gratification. You didn't want to wait for the bigger prize because you set your eyes on the short-term prize, and that's all you could see. You wanted a new toy now, even if you knew you could save your money for a few months and buy the bigger toy that you wanted even more. And that's the kind of thinking that the Motivated person must put aside.

  Those who walk the Motivated path must have the patience to take each step toward their goal rather than skip steps, rush to the end, and later regret not having built a solid foundation for their success.

- **Successful people understand that success may not come quickly or easily, but know that it won't come at all if they quit.** Motivated people do not consider quitting as an option. When they commit to something, they determine to do whatever is necessary to win. To illustrate the point, Jack Canfield was rejected 144 times before he found a publisher for his book, "Chicken Soup for the Soul." When Jack told the publisher that he wanted to sell 1.5 million books in the first 18 months, the publisher laughed and said he'd be lucky to sell 20,000 copies. That first book sold more than 8 million copies in America alone, and 10 million copies worldwide. Canfield's book brand is now a $1 Billion brand! What if Jack had decided to quit when his publisher gave him the news that he'd be lucky to sell 20,000 books?

- **The Motivated influencer doesn't take no for an answer.** When you're a Motivated influencer with a vision for succeeding and helping others, you are not deterred by others saying no to you. You know their opinion is not what's important to your success. You can take their good advice and use it to make improvements to your plan, but you won't take their rejection as the final word. If anything, their rejection will spur you on to greater things.

At the age of 15, after a close family friend died of pancreatic cancer, a young man named Jack Andraka had the idea for creating an earlier detection diagnostic test for pancreatic cancer. His goal was to create a test that would detect pancreatic cancer much earlier. Even though his idea for the test was far superior to those that the billion-dollar pharmaceutical companies had developed, Jack's proposal to develop the test was rejected by 199 research labs. Still, Jack did not give up on his goal and sent out the 200th proposal. It was not until the 200th proposal was presented, that Dr. Anirban Maitra, Professor of Pathology, Oncology and Chemical and Biomolecular Engineering at Johns Hopkins School of Medicine accepted the proposal. Working after school and on weekends at the lab for about seven months, Jack developed the pancreatic test that can provide early detection of 100% of pancreatic, ovarian, and lung cancers. It's probably safe to say that Jack's perseverance became a lifeline for hundreds of thousands of people!

Mark Cuban, billionaire entrepreneur, said, "I've learned that it doesn't matter how many times you failed. You only have to be right once. I tried to sell powdered milk. I was an idiot lots of times, and I learned from them all."

Motivated Thinking from Chapter 15:

- Being able to persevere in the face of life's peaks and valleys is critical to growing and maintaining your Motivated life.
- Progress is what counts!

Part Four: Your New Path

Chapter Sixteen

~

Coping with Misplaced People

"Stay away from negative people. They have a problem for every solution."

~Albert Einstein

In a very inspirational article in MindBodyGreen, titled, "5 Ways To Stay Positive When Negative People Drain Your Energy," writer Rucha Tadwalkar lists 5 ways to help cope with the negative people who find their way into your life. They are:

1. **Don't take it personally.**

Many times, when people are dealing with difficulties in their lives, those around them become the targets of their unhealthy coping strategies. Their behaviors manifest out of insecurities, fears, and anger. The most important thing you can remember is that this is about them, not you, and therefore, don't take it personally.

2. Remain grateful for what is going well.

Make a gratitude list, let people know how thankful you are for their presence, and count your blessings for the small things. Put good energy out into the world in return for all you have been given. **Gratitude** can go a long way in reminding us that life involves more than our immediate surroundings and expands beyond our everyday.

3. Remind yourself that everyone has their own journeys.

We all have to learn different lessons in life. Perhaps this person has come into your life for a reason. At the same time, this person has to come to their own realizations on their own time. Many call this karma. However you view it, when we adopt a broader view, we're able to get out of our limited thinking.

4. View this challenge as an opportunity for growth and self-discovery.

Changing our mindsets can transform our attitudes. Slightly altering your perception can also help you imagine what the other person might be experiencing. You may want to ask yourself, *What is happening in this person's life that is making them behave this way?* We all go through periods of self-doubt and uncertainty. Considering it's difficult to stay positive right after a disappointment or a crisis, it's ideal to cultivate healthy habits while we're feeling good about ourselves. We can take this opportunity to reflect on how we would be affected if we found ourselves in similar circumstances.

5. Spend time alone.

Make time to pursue a hobby, journal, take a walk, or meditate. Giving ourselves time to think can create wonders on our psyches and overall attitudes. Many people underestimate the importance of being alone with our thoughts. Even if you spend the beginning of that time being angry toward this person, it is a necessary step towards shifting your thinking, so that you can return to positivity. When you allow time to process, you give yourself the opportunity to come up with insights and solutions.

Stay Positive and Focused

There's no doubt that as you make positive changes in your own life, you're going to be confronted even more with negative, Misplaced people. Sometimes it feels as though it's the Universe's way of testing our resolve. The key is not to let it interrupt or change your own progress in any way.

Remaining positive and looking for solutions rather than focusing on problems is part of living the Motivated life. Those who remain on the Misplaced path, whether team members, significant other, or family members, can bring constant negativity to your environment. You have probably been subjected to this type of person. They find fault with everything and everyone. They always focus on the problem and do not put much effort into the solution. They are certain that whatever you do will fail. Nothing is ever good enough for the negative Misplaced person. Every word out of their mouth is negative and lands like a dark cloud over every conversation, meeting, project, or event.

Negative team members also have a habit of putting others down and criticizing their work. When this happens, the team may lose confidence and pride of ownership of the project. What's the point in putting forth any effort or continuing a project that won't yield good results?

What can you do if you are unfortunate enough to have to work with a negative team member? First, determine that you will remain positive through all of the negativity. Easier said than done? Perhaps it won't be easy, but keep in mind that remaining positive is a choice. You are not responsible for the negative person's choices, words, or actions, but you are responsible for your own. You can choose each day to be positive no matter what another person chooses.

What do every one of the successful people that you just read about have in common? They tried. They failed. They persevered. They succeeded. They repeated and succeeded again, and again. Success became their way of life. That's the Motivated life!

May you find success and happiness on your new Motivated journey!

Onward...

A Final Message from The Author

~

This book is not about the author, me, it's about you, and for you. I've purposely left myself out of the text because I wanted to put everything that I had into creating something dynamic and helpful for you! However, I think that it's important for you to know where the inspiration for this book arose.

It all comes down to the drive-thru window pictured below.

"Sorry, You're Two Pennies Short"

Years ago, as a young man, I pulled into a drive-thru window at a fast food restaurant in the town where I grew up. It was a late summer night, I had just left work, and I was starving. I was also broke. It wasn't because I wasn't trying, because I was. I just wasn't succeeding at the time, and I wasn't even sure why. You may feel the same way, some days.

After I ordered a very discounted meal, I pulled up to the window that you see in the picture above. There wasn't anyone behind me. It was just me, and a young lady working inside. By the time that I reached the window, I realized that I didn't have quite enough money to pay for my order. But, I thought that I had almost enough, and that I would appeal to the person working at the window for help. I was given my food and I smiled at the young lady whose face showed through the small glass box. I told her that I only had two dollars and five cents with me, even though my bill was two dollars and seven cents. For as long as I live, I'll never forget what happened next. The young lady looked at me, took the food back inside, and just before closing the window said, "sorry, you're two pennies short." I left hungry and humiliated beyond belief.

I've thought a lot about that moment over the years, and I've come to realize that it was a major turning point in my life. When I left the restaurant that night, I drove to a field, got out of car and laid on the ground. I had hit rock bottom. As I looked up at the stars, alone in the world, I remember saying to myself, "I don't want to live like this anymore!" Whatever I have to do to change, and to make sure that nothing like this ever happens to me again, I will do!

I never knew the young lady that took that food back from me, and I didn't know it at the time, but I owe her a huge debt of gratitude. For she lit a fire in me that still burns to this day.

After that night, I was fortunate enough to move in a different direction. I started listening to speakers, studying, and surrounding myself with people that had a different perspective on life. Was it easy, no! Not at all. Many times, I wanted to quit. And yet, because I didn't, I was able to go from living in a mobile home, in a small town in Michigan, to working with major successful executives and leaders in some of the greatest companies in the world. I've been able to live the life of an entrepreneur, travel the world, and make sure that my own family will live a different life. All because, I was two pennies short!

My life isn't perfect, nobody's is, and I still have a lot more to do. But I have continued to evolve and grow, and my hope is that you're doing the same. This book is full of the best timing and strategies that I learned along the way, from people that have produced incredible results in their own life. And, my hope is that you use it to change yours. Wherever you whatever you're doing, only you, and you alone know if you're on a Misplaced path. If you are, and you want to change, YOU CAN! I believe it with all of my heart.

If you find this book helpful, and you would like to let me know, it would be a privilege to hear from you. You can contact me at **motivatedormisplaced@gmail.com.**

-The End-

Further Reading & Planning:

- Bogle, John. *Little Book of Commonsense Investing*. Wiley, 2007.
- Brown, Les. *It's Not Over Until You Win*. Simon & Schuster, 1997.
- Brown, Les. *Laws of Success*. Selby Marketing Associates, 2017.
- Brown, Les. *Live Your Dreams*. Harper Collins, 1992
- Dyer, Wayne. *Change Your Thoughts, Change Your Life*. Hay House, 2009.
- Dyer, Wayne. *Excuses Be Gone*. Hay House, 2011.
- Ferris, Timothy. *The Four-Hour Work Week*. Harmon, 2009.
- Kiyosaki, Robert. *Rich Dad, Poor Dad*. Warner Books Ed., 2000.
- Goldman, Daniel. *Emotional Intelligence*. Bantam Books, 2005.
- Green, Alexander. *The Gone Fishin' Portfolio*. Gildan Media, 2008.
- Hill, Napoleon. *Think and Grow Rich*. The Ralston Society, 1937.
- Nightingale, Earl. *The Strangest Secret*. Merchant Books, 1976.
- Robbins, Tony. *Master The Money Game*. Simon & Schuster, 2014.
- Robbins, Tony. *Unshakeable*. Simon & Schuster, 2017.
- Siegel, Jeremy J. *Stocks for the Long Run: The Definitive Guide to Financial Market Returns & Long-Term Investment Strategies*. McGraw Hill, 2014.
- Tzu, Lao, Translated by Stephen Mitchell. *Tao Te Ching*. Harper Perennial, 1994.
- Various Writings of Warren Buffet.
- Ziglar, Zig. *Goals*. Simon & Schuster, 2002.

Financial Planning Websites and Apps:
- CNBC
- Mint
- Motley Fool
- Personal Capital
- TD Ameritrade

Bibliography:

Cross, Jay. "Informal Learning: Rediscovering the Natural Pathways That Inspire Innovation and Performance. San Francisco." John Wiley & Sons, Inc., 2007.

Gatto, John Taylor and Zlayback, Zachary. "Dumbing Us Down: The Hidden Curriculum of Compulsory Schooling," New Society Publishers, 2017.

Gladwell, Malcolm. "The Tipping Point: How Little Things Can Make a Big Difference." New York: Back Bay Books/Little Brown, and Company. 2002.

https://www.investopedia.com/terms/s/standard-of-living.asp.

US Credit Card Debt by the Numbers. (Mar. 31, 2018). Retrieved from https://www.magnifymoney.com/blog/news/u-s-credit-card-debt-by-the-numbers628618371/.

Average American Saves Less Than 5 Percent-See How You Stack Up. (Aug. 30, 2017). NerdWallet. CNBC MAKEIT. Retrieved from https://www.cnbc.com/2017/08/30/average-american-saves-less-than-5-percent-see-how-you-stack-up.html.

ResMed. Largest Consumer Sleep Study Just Released at CES. (2017). Retrieved from https://www.resmed.com/us/en/technology-partner/newsandinformation/news-releases/2017/largest-consumer-sleep-study-just-released-at-ces-2017.html.

Riley, Melissa Kvidahl. n.d. New Hope Network. Retrieved from http://www.newhope.com/business-resources/how-one-ceo-took-supplement-company-entrepreneurial-inspirational?NL=NP-04&Issue=NP-04_20180511_NP-04_430&sfvc4enews=42&cl=article_2_1&utm_rid=CNHNM000000188348&utm_campaign=25712&utm_medium=email.

Shewan, Dan. Robots Will Destroy Our Jobs and We're Not Ready For It . (Jan. 11, 2017). Retrieved from https://www.theguardian.com/technology/2017/jan/11/robots-jobs-employees-artificial-intelligence.

www.ingramcontent.com/pod-product-compliance
Lightning Source LLC
Chambersburg PA
CBHW030648220526
45463CB00005B/1689